Manga:
Introduction, Challenges,
and Best Practices

Presented by

The Comic Book Legal Defense Fund

Edited by

Melinda Beasi

Contributors

Katherine Dacey

Shaenon Garrity

Sean Gaffney

Ed Chavez

Erica Friedman

Robin Brenner

The Comic Book Legal Defense Fund Presents
Manga: Introduction, Challenges, and Best Practices

This publication made possible thanks to a generous grant from The Gaiman Foundation.

Book layout by Lissa Pattillo

Published by
Dark Horse Books
A division of Dark Horse Comics, Inc.
10956 SE Main Street
Milwaukie, OR 97222
DarkHorse.com

Library of Congress Cataloging-in-Publication Data

Manga : introduction, challenges, and best practices / presented by The Comic Book Legal Defense Fund ; edited by Melinda Beasi ; contributors, Katherine Dacey, Shaenon Garrity, Sean Gaffney, Ed Chavez, Erica Friedman, Robin Brenner. -- First edition.
    pages cm
ISBN 978-1-61655-278-7
1. Comic books, strips, etc.--History and criticism. 2. Popular culture--Japanese influences. 3. Comic books, strips, etc., in education--Handbooks, manuals, etc. I. Beasi, Melinda. II. Comic Book Legal Defense Fund
PN6710.M27 2013
741.5'9--dc23
                    2013035643

First edition: June 2013
10 9 8 7 6 5 4 3 2
Printed in the United States of America

Table of Contents

CHAPTER 1

What Is Manga?

by Katherine Dacey

Section 1: History of Manga in Japan

Manga has deep roots in Japan's painting and printmaking culture, roots that extend as far back as the eleventh century. Some of the earliest surviving sequential narratives have been attributed to Toba Sojo (1053–1140), who painted religious parables on long, narrow scrolls. The most famous of these, the Chojugiga, or "Frolicking Animals," depicts frogs, monkeys, rabbits, cats, and foxes behaving like humans: they pray and wrestle, dress like clerics, and read sacred texts. Toba also painted more explicitly humorous images; his Hohigassen, or "Farting Contest," which dates to the twelfth century, is as bawdy and scatological as the title suggests, documenting the results of a yam-eating contest. These early visual narratives did not use frames or word balloons but the physical structure of the scroll to lead the viewer through the proper sequence of events, making them an early forerunner to contemporary comics.

Until the seventeenth century, however, scroll painting was the exclusive provenance of wealthy individuals and priests. Around 1600, improvements in woodblock printing techniques helped facilitate the growth of modern Japanese print culture in general, and the ukiyo-e print in particular. Popular subjects included geisha, actors, samurai, and other denizens of the pleasure districts, painted in an exaggerated style. In the following centuries, artists expanded the repertoire of images to include a greater range of subjects, from the supernatural to the satirical.

Alongside the growing market for inexpensive prints was an emerging book culture. In 1702, the first compilation of cartoons, Shumboku Ooka's *Tobae Sankokushi*, was printed in Osaka. Such compilations were dubbed *toba-e* in honor of the twelfth-century humorist, and sold briskly in cosmopolitan areas (Schodt 1997:37). Later in the century, another form of sequential narrative, the *kibyoshi* (yellow book), came to prominence, offering readers humorous stories told through a mixture of illustrations and captions. Other books combining text and images included the *eiribon*, or illustrated novel, and the *ukiyo-zoshi*, or floating-world novel, which combined text and *ukiyo*-style prints; like the *toba-e* and the *kibyoshi*, these forms of entertainment were first cultivated in the eighteenth century.

The term *manga* was coined by Katsuhika Hokusai, whose instructional series the *Hokusai Manga* ran from 1814 to 1878. As Hokusai used the term, however, it denoted "whimsical pictures"; the sketches contained within these books were not stories or sequential art, but collections of vividly drawn caricatures, animals, supernatural creatures, and scenes of nature. Not until the twentieth century was the term regularly applied to comics.

Western Influences

The opening of Japan to the West in 1854 by Commodore Matthew Perry had a small but important effect on the development of cartooning in Japan. Two European expatriates—Charles Wirgman, an Englishman, and Georges Bigot, a Frenchman—helped popularize the use of Western-style perspective in caricature. Though Wirgman's *The Japan Punch* (1862–1887) had a tiny circulation, his cartoons were studied and discussed among Japanese artists. The term *ponchi*, derived from the magazine's title, was widely used to describe one-panel cartoons; *ponchi* books, briefly popular in the early Taisho period (1912–1926), were collections of such illustrations.

Also influential was American cartoonist George McManus, whose *Bringing Up Father* was serialized in *Asahi Graph* beginning in 1923 (Schodt 45). The use of frames, panels, and word balloons had antecedents in nineteenth-century Japanese print culture; McManus's strip, however, helped popularize these conventions on a much wider scale. *Bringing Up Father* also sparked a fad for American comic strips; in the 1920s, such all-American staples as *Felix the Cat, The Katzenjammer Kids*, and *Mutt and Jeff* also appeared in Japanese newspapers.

Emergence of Modern Manga

Modern manga—long-form stories spanning hundreds or thousands of pages—can be traced to the 1920s and 1930s in Japan. Children's magazines such as *Shōnen Club* (founded in 1914) and *Shōjo Club* (founded in 1923) contained a mixture of short stories, articles, illustrations, and comics. The most popular comic series were reprinted in hardbound books, in much the same fashion as contemporary manga are reprinted today in paperback trades. Among the most popular titles during this early phase in manga history were Suiho Tagawa's *Norakuro,* which chronicled the exploits of a small black dog who joins the military; Gajo Sakamoto's *Tank Tankuro,* an early example of "mecha" or giant-robot manga; and Shimada Keizo's *Dankichi the Adventurer,* which scholar Michael Weiner likens to Hergé's *Tintin* (Weiner 114).

Though newspapers and magazines helped popularize manga, *kamishibai,* or paper-theater shows, also played a role in the medium's development in the 1930s and 1940s, both as a popularizer of long-form storytelling and as an incubator of talent. At the height of its popularity, nearly five million people attended a *kamishibai* performance every day (Nash 15). *Kamishibai* were, essentially, serials with sound effects provided by a live performer (the *kamishibai-ya*) who, each day, would set up his wooden theater in a neighborhood park and deliver a new installment of a popular series, using a sequence of ten to twenty prepainted panels to aid him.

One of the most obvious corollaries between the manga and *kamishibai* industries was their careful appeal to gender and age. As in the publishing world, the *kamishibai* industry produced different stories for boys (*shōnen*) and girls (*shōjo*); *shōnen kamishibai* were more likely to be action oriented or fantastic in nature, while *shōjo kamishibai* focused on everyday experiences. Some of the most popular *kamishibai* stories—*Golden Bat,* which featured a masked superhero, and *Kitaro of the Graveyard,* which focused on the world of *yokai,* or demons—enjoyed a second life in print as the heroes of *shōnen* manga.

Kamishibai was also an important training ground for many postwar manga artists. Based in Osaka, the *kamishibai* industry used an assembly-line process to produce paintings and scripts; some workers drew outlines, others supplied color, and still others wrote story lines. Three of Japan's most influential manga artists and writers—Shigeru Mizuki, author of *GeGeGe no Kitaro*; Sanpei Shirato, author of *Kamui Den*, and Kazuo Koike, author of *Lone Wolf and Cub*— all labored in the *kamishibai* industry before moving into manga publishing in the 1950s.

In the immediate aftermath of World War II, there was explosive growth in the *akahon*—literally, "red book"—market. Osaka was also the heart of the *akahon* publishing industry, cranking out hundreds of cheap books for children. A typical *akahon* consisted of 24–48 pages, trimmed to the size of a postcard, and retailed for about 50 yen. Like American comic books, *akahon* were not generally sold in bookstores, but at newsstands, candy stores, and festivals. Even cheaper editions— called *zokkibon* or *mikiribon*—were also available through the same alternative distribution channels; these disposable books were usually unauthorized editions of popular works, printed on even lower-quality paper.

Osamu Tezuka's *New Treasure Island*, published in 1947, was one of the *akahon* market's first commercial successes, selling nearly 400,000 copies. Tezuka's work was notable both for its length and for the sophistication of its cartooning; the opening pages, which featured a lengthy scene of a car speeding over a curving roadway, offered a moviegoing experience in paper form. Publishers raced to capitalize on *New Treasure Island*'s success with their own look-alike comics. In fact, a culture of copying pervaded the industry; popular movies, novels, comic strips, and Western cartoon characters were all fodder for *akahon* stories.

As the cost of *akahon* began rising in the 1950s, rental libraries became a more popular way for young readers to enjoy manga. Instead of paying 100 yen for a book, readers could pay a more modest ten to rent a single volume. Rental libraries proved popular with teenagers and young adults as well. In an effort to cater to this emerging audience, publishers launched two magazines aimed at older patrons: *Kage* (Shadow), which debuted in 1956, and *Machi* (Street), which debuted in 1957. The stories in *Kage* and *Machi* covered a variety of genres, including true crime and samurai dramas. These magazines took their artistic inspiration from the world of movies, emphasizing realism and cinematic use of angle and light to convey motion. *Akahon* publishers also courted older readers with titles such as Sanpei Shirato's *Ninja bugeichō* (*Ninja Combat Scrolls*, 1959), a seventeen-volume sword-and-sandal epic that proved immensely popular among high-school and college students; nearly 2.5 million library patrons read *Ninja bugeichō* during its initial publication (Isao 147).

Weekly manga magazines also became an increasingly important vehicle for comics. Though the first of these weeklies—*Weekly Shōnen Sunday* and *Weekly Shōnen Magazine*—appeared in 1959, it wasn't until the mid-1960s that many of them jettisoned their traditional mixture of articles, photos, and comics in favor of an exclusive manga emphasis. The other great innovation of the period was formatting: in the 1960s, publishers introduced a "phone book" style publication that was cheap to produce and sold primarily through train station kiosks and newsstands. The low cost and widespread availability of such magazines helped make manga a favorite reading material for commuters of all ages, and inspired publishers to develop more specialized magazines for adults in the 1970s and 1980s.

By the 1980s, manga was one of the largest and most lucrative sectors of the publishing industry; of the five billion books published in Japan in 1984, for example, more than one in four was a volume of manga (Schodt 1997:12). Popular magazines such as *Shōnen Jump* reached as many as 2.6 million readers weekly, while series such as Akira Toriyama's *Dr. Slump* sold as many as three million copies per volume (Schodt 1997:14). The manga market's robust growth continued through the early 1990s, reaching peak sales in 1995. That year, over 1.34 billion manga magazines were sold—a figure the industry would never match again. (In 2007, by contrast, only 745 million manga magazines were sold, a decline of more than 40%.) (Wiseman)

The arrival of the cell phone and the shrinking youth market are two of the biggest reasons for manga publishing's slumping sales. The once-ubiquitous phone book magazine is being supplanted to an extent by cell phone manga; between 2005 and 2006 alone, phone manga sales figures doubled from $39 million to nearly $80 million (Wiseman). Electronic devices also provide commuters a wealth of alternatives to manga, from video games to streaming content and cell phone novels.

Declining birth rates, too, are exacerbating the problem. At the beginning of the twentieth-century manga boom, in 1950, 35.4% of Japan's population was fourteen or younger. These readers eagerly embraced titles like *New Treasure Island*, and as they "aged out" of *shōnen* and *shōjo* manga, they continued to read comics, prompting additional growth in the areas of *seinen* (men's) and *josei* (women's) manga. In 2006, however, the pool of new manga readers had shrunk considerably: just 13.6% of the population was fourteen or younger (Wiseman).

The manga industry's tried-and-true method of hooking young readers, then providing them with new material for each stage of their lives, faces a considerable threat from this change in demographics.

Major Marketing Demographics

The manga market in Japan is divided into several major categories, each determined by the age and gender of the target audience. The best-selling category, *shōnen*, is aimed at boys ten and older, though *shōnen* manga are read by girls and adults as well. *Shōjo*, or manga for a young female readership, is written for girls ten and older; historically, *shōjo* has had less crossover appeal for male readers, as many *shōjo* titles focus on romantic relationships, even when the ostensible genre is fantasy, science fiction, or sports. *Seinen*, or manga for young men, is a more recent phenomenon, dating to the early 1960s, while *josei*, or manga for young women, is the newest of the four major categories, with the first *josei* magazines debuting in 1980.

Sequential Art and Animation

The synergy between animation and comics in Japan began in the postwar period. In the late 1950s, as the Japanese economy recovered from World War II, Toei Studios began releasing feature-length movies based on Asian folklore and Western fairy tales. One of Toei's first films was *Boku no Son Gokū* (released in English as *Alakazam the Great*), an animated retelling of the Chinese epic *Journey to the West*. The source material for *Boku*, however, was not the classical text, but a manga version by Osamu Tezuka, making *Boku* one of the very first anime to have a comic-book analog.

Following the success of *Boku*, Tezuka formed Mushi Studios in 1961 with the intent of developing animated programs for television. Mushi's first project was an adaptation of Tezuka's *Astro Boy*, which had been running in the pages of *Shōnen* magazine since 1952. *Astro Boy* debuted on Fuji TV in 1963, and was a certifiable hit. The animation was crude by contemporary standards: it was black and white, and frequently recycled background elements as a cost- and labor-saving measure. But its popularity helped pave the way for subsequent manga adaptations such as *Gigantor* (1963–1966), based on Mitsuteru Yokoyama's *Tetsujin 28-go*; *Kimba the White Lion* (1965–1966), based on Tezuka's *Jungle Emperor Leo*; *Sally the Witch* (1966–68), based on a *shōjo* manga by Yokoyama; and *Mach GoGoGo!* (1967–68), based on a *shōnen* manga by Tatsuo Yoshida (and better known to English-speaking audiences as *Speed Racer*).

Though the first wave of animated shows was aimed at younger viewers, programs for older teens began to appear alongside more child-friendly fare in the 1970s. *Seinen* manga *Lupin III*, which followed the exploits of a randy jewel thief, was one such comic to make the leap from page to screen in 1971; Go Nagai's horror series *Devilman*, which debuted as an animated show in 1972, was another early example. Over the next ten years, animated shows based on manga became an increasingly visible element of Japanese programming, with the most dramatic period of growth occurring in the 1980s and 1990s. Today, anime is a staple of Japanese television, offering the same range of genres and approaches represented in the world of manga publishing.

Feature-length films based on manga and OVAs, or "original video animations," are another important manifestation of the manga-anime relationship. Many of these projects do not strictly adhere to the source material, but are conceived as an extension of the original story, placing characters in new situations, or introducing new characters not seen in the manga's print run. In 1980, for example, Toho Studios released a film based on Fujiko F. Fujio's *Doraemon*. The film was commercially successful, prompting Toho to release a new *Doraemon* feature every year; though the characters and setup are clearly drawn from the manga, the film plots are more action driven than gag oriented, and take place in a variety of settings: outer space, underwater, the Triassic period.

OVAs date to the VCR era. Though Mamoru Oshii's *Dallos* (1983), the first OVA, was not based on a manga, other straight-to-video releases were. The category remained strong through the 1980s, then experienced a period of stagnation until the introduction of the DVD. In the last ten years, animation studios have revived the practice in myriad forms, releasing some series exclusively in DVD format, or withholding material from the original television run for inclusion in the DVD release.

Given the ubiquity of anime on television and in movie theaters, it should come as no surprise that many successful anime spawn their own manga series. *Tenchi Muyo!*, a popular OVA of the early 1990s, was one such example; in 1994, two years after the first OVA was released, Hitoshi Okuda was hired by *Comic Dragon Jr.* magazine to adapt the story into a manga. The manga proved popular enough to run for six years, resulting in twelve volumes. A more recent trend involves the near-simultaneous launch of an anime and manga franchise. *Puella Magi Madoka Magica*, which made its television debut in January 2011, has three different manga tie-ins currently in print, one of which was released just a month after the series began airing.

~ ~ ~ ~ ~ ~ ~ ~ ~ ~

Section 2: Manga's Journey to the West

Though animated Japanese shows began airing in the United States as early as 1963, when NBC began syndication of *Astro Boy*, manga is a newer phenomenon, making its stateside debut in the late 1970s. The first manga to be published in English at length was *Barefoot Gen*, Keiji Nakazawa's semiautobiographical account of the Hiroshima bombing. *Barefoot Gen* was followed in 1987 by Kazuo Koike and Goseki Kojima's *Lone Wolf and Cub*, which was released by First Comics, and by a trio of comics from Viz: Kaoru Shintani's *Area 88*, Sanpei Shirato's *Legend of Kamui*, and Kazuya Kudo and Ryoichi Ikegami's *Mai the Psychic Girl*.

The American manga market's initial growth was slow. In the years between *Barefoot Gen*'s release and the revised edition of Frederik Schodt's seminal work *Manga! Manga!*, only 100 or so titles had been translated into English (Schodt 1997:7). By the late 1990s, however, the category was beginning to grow in importance, thanks, in part, to anime's increased presence on American cable television; thousands of readers were introduced to manga such as *Bleach, Dragonball, InuYasha, Naruto*, and *Sailor Moon* through their animated adaptations. The other key to manga's success was the publishers' decision to rely less on the direct market—the traditional distribution network for American comics—and more on chain stores such as Barnes & Noble, Borders, and Walmart, where *Bleach* and *Sailor Moon* fans were more likely to shop. By 2006, manga had become one of the fastest-growing sectors of the American publishing industry, inspiring media outlets such as the

New York Times, Time, USA Today, and the *Wall Street Journal* to publish articles about the American "manga boom."

Three companies were most responsible for popularizing manga with American readers: Dark Horse Comics, Viz Media, and Tokyopop. Dark Horse, founded in 1986, began publishing manga in 1988; their *Oh My Goddess!* is currently the longest-running manga in North America. Historically, the Dark Horse catalog has emphasized science fiction, action, and horror, though in recent years Dark Horse has expanded its manga imprint to include *shōjo* titles such as CLAMP's *Cardcaptor Sakura, Clover*, and *Magic Knight Rayearth*.

Viz Media was also founded in 1986 with funding from Japanese publisher Shogakukan, releasing its first titles the following year. Viz reorganized in 2002, when Shueisha, a major Japanese publisher, also invested in the company. Over the last ten years, Viz has become the largest North American publisher of manga, with a diverse catalog that runs the gamut from children's titles such as *Leave It to PET!* to ultraviolent *seinen* manga such as *Black Lagoon*.

Tokyopop, originally known as Mixx, was founded in 1997. Tokyopop is best known for helping introduce a standard trade paperback size for American manga, making it easier for retailers to shelve manga alongside conventional books. Tokyopop was also instrumental in popularizing *shōjo* manga with American readers; prior to the publication of *Sailor Moon* in 1997, most North American companies published *shōnen* and *seinen* manga, licensing series that most closely mirrored the kind of stories being sold in comic shops: horror, action, science fiction. At its peak in the mid-2000s, Tokyopop was the second-largest distributor of manga in North America, though a series of reversals—including the loss of valuable licenses from Japanese publisher Kodansha—eventually led to the company's near disappearance in 2011. (A German branch of the company continues to license manga for the European market, and the U.S. website, updated in late 2012, offers a limited selection of manga as ebooks and print-on-demand.)

In the late 1990s and early 2000s, all three companies tried to launch their own manga magazines, taking their inspiration from Japanese publications such as *Nakayoshi, Big Comic Spirits*, and *Weekly Shōnen Jump*. Dark Horse, for example, launched *Super Manga Blast* in 2000, featuring work by Makoto Kobayashi (*Club*

9, What's Michael?) and Mohiro Kitoh (*Shadow Star*), while Tokyopop used *MixxZine* to introduce readers to *Parasyte, Magic Knight Rayearth,* and *Sailor Moon.* Viz also experimented with magazines such as *Manga Vizion, Animerica Extra, Shojo Beat,* and *PULP.* Today, only one of these magazines—Viz's *Shōnen Jump*—still exists, though Viz abandoned its monthly print edition in favor of a weekly digital version in 2011.

In the early 2000s, a number of companies entered the field, but by 2008, the sector's growth had slowed, and competition for the most desirable properties was beginning to price smaller firms out of the market. By 2010, fewer publishers remained in the business, as the manga market continued to contract. Currently, Viz, Dark Horse, Digital Manga Publishing, and two newcomers—Kodansha Comics (2008) and Yen Press (2006)—dominate the North American market. Other important publishers include Seven Seas, an imprint of Tor Books; Vertical, Inc., a publisher specializing in manga and Japanese novels; and Drawn & Quarterly, a Canadian company that has licensed work by Yoshihiro Tatsumi and Shigeru Mizuki.

Digital distribution of manga—online and via apps—has become an increasingly important element of most publishers' marketing strategies. Dark Horse, Viz, and Yen Press were among the first companies to introduce iPad/iPhone-compatible editions of popular manga, while companies such as Digitial Manga Publishing experimented with electronic manga rentals. JManga, an online subscription service, was launched in 2011 by a consortium of small Japanese manga publishers; although notable for the diversity of its offerings, which include a number of subgenres that are not well represented in English translation, it ceased operations in early 2013.

Manga's Influence on Western Pop Culture

It's difficult to fully gauge manga's influence outside of Japan, as anime, video games, and toys have also played a role in introducing Westerners to Japanese popular culture. One of the most visible manifestations of manga's influence, however, is in the rise of a North American "*otaku*" subculture focused primarily on anime and manga. Over the last twenty years, Internet forums, manga-focused blogs, and conventions have helped nurture this fan community; Anime Expo, held annually in California since 1992, regularly sponsors manga-themed panels and cosplay contests. Comic conventions were slower to embrace manga fans, though manga publishers and panels have become staples of San Diego and New York Comic Con, respectively. In 2010, for example, *shōjo* manga pioneer Moto Hagio attended San Diego Comic-Con, where she signed autographs, received an Inkpot Award, and was interviewed onstage by manga scholar Matt Thorn.

Manga has also helped familiarize the American public with visual tropes that appear in Japanese pop culture: the cute simplification of *Pokémon*, for example, being among the most well known. One of the most obvious manifestations of this influence is in the world of children's animation. A quick look at Nickelodeon and Cartoon Network's recent hits, for example, yields shows such as *Hi Hi Puffy Ami Yumi, Ben 10, Avatar: The Last Airbender,* and *The Legend of Korra*, all of which draw inspiration from the visual language of anime and manga.

Last but not least, manga is influencing American comics culture. Many fine-art schools are now offering degrees in sequential art, in part because of growing interest in manga and anime, while an emerging generation of artists—including Svetlana Chmakova and Felipe Smith—have developed personal styles that are an amalgamation of Western and Japanese storytelling conventions. (For further discussion of such East-West cross-pollination, see discussion of original English-language manga on page 18.)

~ ~ ~ ~ ~ ~ ~ ~ ~

Section 3: What's Not Manga

In an effort to expand their market share and to find less expensive sources of material, many American publishers have licensed or commissioned other types of graphic novels that are similar in presentation to manga, but originate from countries other than Japan. The three most common types are *manhua*, or comics published in Hong Kong or Taiwan; *manhwa*, or comics published in South Korea; and original English-language manga (OEL manga), mangainfluenced comics originating from English-speaking countries such as the United States, Great Britain, or Australia.

Manhua

Of the three categories, the least common is *manhua*, or Chinese-language comics. *Manhua* followed a similar developmental trajectory as manga, originating first in a vibrant fin-de-siècle print culture in Shanghai, and was further developed in Hong Kong and Taiwan after the Communist revolution in China. As in Japan, a variety of different illustrated book traditions— including the *lianhuanhua* and the *xiaoshu*—eventually gave rise to an indigenous form of sequential art that fused Chinese illustration styles with Western-style cartoon panels. Early *manhua* plots drew inspiration from myriad sources, from ancient Chinese history to Beijing opera.

Manhua first appeared in the United States in the late 1980s courtesy of Jademan Comics, a Hong Kong company eager to expand its reach across the Pacific. Jademan Comics focused primarily on historical and martials-arts *manhua*, publishing English-language editions of series such as *Chinese Hero, Force of Buddha's Palm,* and *Drunken Fist.* In 1993, Jademan Comics licensed part of its catalog to another company, DRMaster, before withdrawing from the American market. Since DRMaster's demise, only two major American publishers, Tokyopop and Yen Press, have licensed *manhua* on a sporadic basis.

What has been translated into English tends to fall into one of three categories: *manhua* for young female readers, chosen for its visual and thematic similarities to *shōjo* manga; martial-arts stories that bear a strong resemblance to *wuxia* films; and experimental comics that defy easy categorization. The vast majority of licensed *manhua* fall into the second category, with historical settings that provide ample opportunities for sword fights and hand-to-hand combat. A few more Westernized *manhua* have been published in English, the most notable of which were Zhang Bin's *Orange* and *Remember*, two full-color, photorealistic graphic novels about young people in crisis.

Manhwa

More common are *manhwa*, or comics originally published in South Korea. Though there are similarities between *manhwa* and manga's development—such as the importance of postwar rental libraries in cultivating young audiences—censorship has played a larger role in Korean comics than in Japanese. One of the subtler effects of censorship was artistic isolation and stagnation. Korea experienced a brief *shōjo* manga boom in the 1970s, when pirates flooded the Korean market with unauthorized versions of popular Japanese titles. After the government cracked down on Japanese imports, however, Korean artists who had drawn inspiration from *shōjo* pioneers such as Riyoko Ikeda no longer had access to current *shōjo* manga; as a result, variations on the starry-eyed heroines and long-haired princes of 1970s manga flourished in Korea long after they'd fallen out of fashion in Japan.

Today, however, there is a flourishing comics culture in Korea, both in print and online, in a diverse range of styles and genres. More Korean artists are finding an audience for their work outside the country, with major Japanese and American publishers hiring *manhwa* artists to develop series for Japanese and English-speaking readerships. One of the first such crossover hits was In-Wan You and Kyung-Il Yang's *Shin Angyō Onshi* (translated as *Blade of the Phantom Master*), a dark, violent adaptation of *The Legend of Chun Hyang*, a Korean epic. *Shin Angyō Onshi* was simultaneously serialized in Korean magazine *Young Champ* and the Japanese magazine *Monthly Sunday Gene-X* from 2001 to 2007, and proved popular enough to inspire a feature-length film, *Phantom Master: Dark Hero from the Ruined Empire* (2004). *March Story*, written by Hyang-Min Kim and illustrated by Kyung-Il Yang, is another example; since 2008, *March Story* has been running in the pages of *Sunday GX*, a *seinen* manga magazine published by Shogakukan.

Webtoons—or free, online *manhwa*—have become an increasingly important platform for launching new series and cultivating readership, thanks, in part, to the popularity of smartphone technology in Korea. Doha's *The Great Catsby* is one of the best-known examples. *Catsby* originally appeared online in 2005, then was published in book form and adapted for television and the stage. Though webtoons have yet to gain traction in the U.S. market, iSeeToon, a Korea-based company, recently unveiled a webtoon app for American readers.

One of the most important differences between manga and *manhwa* is the limited role of animation in extending or reimagining popular Korean comics. Though there is some synergy between *manhwa* and animation, popular *manhwa* are much more likely to be adapted into television shows featuring real actors. *Goong*, a popular "K-drama" from 2006, is a telling example: it began its life as a *sunjeong*—or girls' *manhwa*—before inspiring two live-action television shows, one a faithful adaptation of the original story, the other a spinoff telling a similar rags-to-riches story about a commoner who marries royalty. Though *Goong* has found a small but appreciative audience in the United States, the television show has done little to increase awareness of the *manhwa* on which it's based—a stark contrast with animated shows such as *Sailor Moon* and *InuYasha*, both of which stimulated considerable American interest in the manga on which those series were based.

Although making a brief debut in North America in the late 1980s, *manhwa* started being licensed in earnest in the early 2000s by companies such as ADV Manga, Dark Horse Comics, Infinity Studios, and Tokyopop. As with other forms of Asian comics in translation, titles were generally chosen for their perceived similarity with successful manga series, with the greatest emphasis on slick martial-arts stories (*Heavenly Executioner Chiwoo, Chun Rhang Yur Jun, Shaman Warrior*), romances (*I.N.V.U., 13th Boy, Narration of Love at 17*), and historical fantasies (*Land of Silver Rain, PhD: Phantasy Degree*). Some specialty publishers have released literary *manhwa*; NBM/ComicsLit published Seyeong-O's *Buja's Diary* and Byun Byung-Jun's *Run, Bong-gu, Run!*, while First Second released Kim Dong Hwa's *Color* trilogy. Additionally, EComix, a Korean publisher, launched an American subsidiary, NETCOMICS, in 2006. Though NETCOMICS originally offered both print and online *manhwa* (as well as manga), NETCOMICS abandoned its print line in favor of low-cost digital comics around 2010.

Of the American companies that published *manhwa* in the early-to-mid 2000s, only Yen Press is still releasing a substantial amount of Korean comics in translation. Some of those titles Yen acquired through iceKunion, a smaller, *manhwa*-focused publisher that Yen absorbed in 2007. Other titles—*Jack Frost, Raiders*, and *One Fine Day* among them—are more recent additions to the Yen Press catalog, signaling the company's continued commitment to translating Korean comics for the American market.

OEL Manga and Manga-Influenced Comics

During the height of the manga boom, Tokyopop and other American manga publishers began championing what came to be known as original English-language (OEL) manga, or manga-influenced comics produced by American, British, and Australian authors. Before the term "OEL manga" was widely adopted, fans and publishers used a number of terms to describe such comics, including Amerimanga, global manga, world manga, and international manga. As with the term manga itself, OEL manga could denote a variety of genres and storytelling approaches, from original stories rendered in a mixture of Western and Japanese styles to adaptations of English-language novels drawn in a generic "manga style."

Japanese influence on American comics can be traced back to the late 1970s and early '80s, with Wendy Pini's art on *Elfquest* and Frank Miller's on *Daredevil*. First Comics later published a Japan-influenced comic, Doug Rice's *Dynamo Joe* (1986–1988), a story about human soldiers who piloted giant robots. Antarctic Press, founded in 1987, was another OEL manga pioneer, publishing two of the longest-running comics in this category: Ben Dunn's *Ninja High School* (1987–present), a broad parody of *shōnen* manga conventions, and Fred Perry's *Gold Digger* (1992–present), a time-traveling adventure series starring a buxom scientist. Other long-running examples of OEL manga include Stan Sakai's *Usagi Yojimbo*, which first appeared in 1987, and Fred Gallagher's *Megatokyo*, which debuted online in 2000, and was subsequently published by several different companies, including CMX Manga (a now-defunct imprint of DC Comics) and Dark Horse Comics.

In the 1990s and 2000s, publishers sought new ways to capitalize on growing awareness of and interest in manga. Tokyopop, for example, launched the Rising Stars of Manga contest in 2002; winning entries were published in a single volume, and several—including Mike Schwark and Ron Kaulfersch's *Van Von Hunter* (2005–2006) and Lindsay Cibos and Jared Hodges's *Peach Fuzz* (2005–2007)—netted their creators deals for three-volume series. Seven Seas also announced an ambitious "global manga" program in the mid-2000s in which American writers collaborated with Asian artists to produce original, manga-influenced comics such as *Blade for Barter* (2005), *Captain Nemo* (2006), *Amazing Agent Luna* (2005–present), and *Aoi House* (2005–2009).

Another important trend in OEL manga is adapting popular young-adult novels into comic book form. In 2006, for example, Tokyopop announced a partnership with HarperCollins that resulted in "manga" versions of such YA franchises as Erin Hunter's *Warriors* and Ellen Schrieber's *Vampire Kisses*, while the now-defunct

Del Rey Manga commissioned a manga based on Dean Koontz's *Odd Thomas* novels. With a few exceptions, such "manga" adaptations have performed well, even cracking the *New York Times* graphic bestseller lists. Currently, Yen Press is the dominant player in this field, with adaptations of James Patterson's *Maximum Ride, Witch & Wizard,* and *Daniel X*, Stephenie Meyer's *Twilight* franchise, and Cecily von Ziegesar's *Gossip Girl* books.

Perhaps the greatest testament to manga's influence on American culture is the emergence of a generation of artists whose work freely mixes Western and Japanese storytelling conventions, creating a unique synthesis of these two traditions. Svetlana Chmakova, creator of *Dramacon* (2005–2007; Tokyopop) and *Nightschool* (2009–2010; Yen Press), is one such example: her character designs and layouts suggest the influence of *shōjo* and *shōnen* manga, yet the characters themselves and the settings in which these stories unfold are clearly Western. Equally striking is Felipe Smith, an American artist who broke into the fiercely competitive Japanese market with *Peepo Choo* (2009), a blistering satire of American *otaku* culture. Smith's work is an amalgamation of influences: video games, *hentai* (pornographic manga), gangster movies, superflat imagery, and anime. Though Smith's work invites comparison with *seinen* manga, the results defy easy categorization, as the prevailing spirit is neither fully Japanese nor fully Western.

~ ~ ~ ~ ~ ~ ~ ~ ~

Section 4: Suggested Reading

Over the last thirty years, scholars, artists, journalists, librarians, and industry professionals have contributed to the growing body of English-language literature on manga. These books run the gamut from how-to manuals for aspiring artists to scholarly treatises on gender roles in *shōjo* manga. Below is a brief overview of resources for the librarian, parent, or teacher seeking more information about manga, whether they're interested in the medium's history or the content of a specific series.

General Overviews

Frederik Schodt has done more than almost any other American writer in explaining manga's origins and place in Japanese culture. Schodt was a friend and assistant to

Osamu Tezuka, translating several of Tezuka's works into English and writing three books about manga for American audiences. Schodt's groundbreaking *Manga! Manga! The World of Japanese Comics* was first published in 1983, when manga was a minimal presence in American comic shops, and revised again in 1997, as more publishers were beginning to enter the field. *Manga! Manga!* was the first book to offer English-speaking readers an introduction to Japanese comics and creators; though the second edition remains in print, the book does not explore the global manga market, and predates the impact of the Internet on distribution and consumption of manga, in or outside Japan.

Schodt's other books include *Dreamland Japan: Writings on Modern Manga*, which was published in 1996, and the more recent *The Astro Boy Essays: Osamu Tezuka, Mighty Atom, and the Manga/Anime Revolution*, released in 2007. Like *Manga! Manga!*, the information in *Dreamland Japan* is now historical rather than contemporary, though Schodt's analyses of specific genres and authors remain useful for anyone wishing to develop a more complete picture of the industry. *The Astro Boy Essays* focuses more explicitly on Schodt's friend Tezuka, exploring the Astro Boy phenomenon through a variety of lenses. Readers interested in the globalization of anime and manga will find *The Astro Boy Essays* a particularly insightful work.

Paul Gravett's *Manga: 60 Years of Japanese Comics*, a more recent addition to manga's body of literature, is a worthy successor to Schodt's *Manga! Manga!* Gravett provides a historical overview of manga's development in the twentieth century, giving particular emphasis to the four primary categories of manga—shōnen, shōjo, seinen, josei—as well as more experimental forms. Since its publication in 2004, many of the examples in this generously illustrated book have been licensed for the English-speaking market, making it a useful text for parents, librarians, and educators wishing to learn more about contemporary manga.

Other titles of interest include Brigitte Koyama-Richard's *One Thousand Years of Manga*. Published in 2008, Koyama-Richard's book offers a somewhat different perspective on manga's development, focusing heavily on manga's origins in Japanese scroll making and print culture. (Readers who find her approach congenial may wish to look for the 2010 companion volume, *Japanese Animation: From Painted Scrolls to Pokémon*.) For readers more interested in manga's history in the

English-speaking world, Jason Yadao's *The Rough Guide to Manga*, published in 2009, offers a helpful introduction. The most useful section of the book focuses on the American manga industry, providing brief but informative descriptions of every publisher whose catalog then included manga. (Note that many of the publishers described in Yadao's book have since folded.) *The Rough Guide to Manga* also offers a list of fifty important manga available in English translation, providing detailed plot summaries for each, and an explanation of their artistic or historical significance.

Readers seeking information on individual artists will find Helen McCarthy's *The Art of Osamu Tezuka: God of Manga* a lively and colorful introduction to the most admired *mangaka* of the twentieth century. McCarthy explores Tezuka's career as an illustrator and animator, devoting chapters to each major phase in Tezuka's artistic development. Another artist-focused work is Tim Lehmann's *Manga: Masters of the Art*. Published in 2005, this anthology includes twelve in-depth interviews with manga artists. Interviewees run the gamut from Takehiko Inoue, whose *Slam Dunk* sold over 120 million copies in Japan in the 1990s, to Erika Sakurazawa, a pioneer in the field of *josei*. Lehmann's interviews focus primarily on the craft of writing comics, and are complemented by numerous images of works in progress.

The globalization of manga is still an emerging field of scholarship in the U.S., with the majority of writing in the area being done by scholars such as Anne Allison, Wendy Siuyi Wong, and Wendy Goldberg. *Japan Pop! Inside the World of Japanese Popular Culture* was one of the first collections of academic essays on Japanese cross-cultural exchange. Though it shows its age—it was published in 2000—the book includes several worthwhile essays on the arrival of anime and manga in America. More problematic is Roland Kelts's *Japanamerica: How Japanese Pop Culture Has Invaded the U.S.*, which was released to wide acclaim in 2006, the height of the manga boom. Though *Japanamerica* is not explicitly focused on manga, Kelts's book offers an impressionistic study of how Japanese video games, animation, and comics have been influencing recent trends in American entertainment. As with many of the books discussed in this section, *Japanamerica* is also somewhat dated, as it alludes to a number of Hollywood projects that never came to fruition. Most recent is *Manga: An Anthology of Global and Cultural Perspectives*, edited by Toni Johnson-Woods and published in 2010. Like *Japan Pop!*, *Manga: An Anthology of Global and Cultural Perspectives* addresses manga's history in Japan and abroad in a more explicitly academic fashion. Readers will find numerous articles on the medium itself, as well as on individual artists and works; mileage will vary according to the reader's familiarity with manga, and willingness to read texts that are sometimes expressed in specialized academic language.

Periodicals

Though the last twenty years has witnessed the launch of many manga and Japanese pop-culture magazines for American readers, only one remains in print today: *Otaku USA,* published bimonthly by Sovereign/Homestead Media. As its title suggests, *Otaku USA* explores the world of Japanese culture with regular features on games, collectibles, cosplay, anime, and manga. The magazine publishes manga reviews, industry news, and generous previews from yet-to-be-released titles.

In the world of scholarship, *Mechademia,* a journal published by University of Minnesota Press, is an important outlet for discussing manga's impact on Western culture. Like the more explicitly fan-oriented *Otaku USA, Mechademia* offers a variety of articles on Japanese popular culture; recent volumes have examined manga, anime, video games, fan communities, and cosplay through a variety of disciplinary lenses, from anthropology to comparative literature. The seventh volume, slated for release this year, explores the theme of "lines of sight," while the eighth, scheduled for a fall 2013 release, will reexamine Osamu Tezuka's career.

For Librarians, Educators, and Parents

Anyone wishing to know more about translated manga will find Jason Thompson's *Manga: The Complete Guide* an indispensable addition to their library. Published in 2007, *Manga: The Complete Guide* offers brief synopses of every manga published in English at the time, with information about the work's original publication history, age rating, and content. (All titles are evaluated on a scale of 0 to 4 stars.) Thompson's guide also provides overviews of such major genres as sports manga, horror, and science fiction, as well as profiles of some of Japan's most famous manga artists. The final two sections of the book focus on manga for adult audiences (*yaoi* and *hentai*), and may prove useful to librarians in determining whether a book is appropriate for their general collection.

In addition to Thompson's excellent—if somewhat dated—book, there are a growing number of resources written by librarians for parents and other library science professionals. Teen librarian Robin Brenner has written one of the most comprehensive and user-friendly of these guides, *Understanding Manga and Anime*. Brenner's book includes an overview of manga and anime's history and a glossary of common Japanese terms. Of particular interest to parents and librarians are Brenner's reading lists; she explores a number of popular genres, providing age recommendations and information about potentially controversial content.

Two newer books covering similar ground are Elizabeth Kalen's *Mostly Manga: A Genre Guide to Popular Manga, Manhwa, Manhua, and Anime* and Snow Wildsmith and Scott Robin's *A Parent's Guide to Choosing the Best Kids' Comics*. As the title of Kalen's book indicates, *Mostly Manga* is written primarily for acquisition librarians. Kalen's book is unusual in its inclusion of *manhwa* and *manhua*, two graphic traditions that are not well represented in the English-language literature on comics. Wildsmith and Robin's book, on the other hand, is expressly intended for parents. Though not manga focused, it does contain age ratings and plot summaries for several popular manga series—a valuable aid to any parent trying to decide if a book is appropriate for her son or daughter.

CHAPTER 2

Shōnen Manga
by Shaenon Garrity

Although manga exists to cater to every conceivable demographic, *shōnen* manga, aimed at grade-school boys, is easily the largest of the four major categories.

~ ~ ~ ~ ~ ~ ~ ~ ~

Section 1: History

The roots of *shōnen* manga can be traced to the comics features in children's magazines in the early decades of the 20th century. In the 1930s, in the pages of the boys' magazine *Shōnen Club*, some of Japan's first popular cartoon characters appeared: Norakuro, a bumbling dog who rises up the ranks of the army of the Dog Nation in Suihō Tagawa's manga *Norakuro* (Black Stray), and Dankichi, a boy who becomes king of a tropical island and introduces the natives to Japanese civilization in Shimada Keizō's *Bōken Dankichi* (Dankichi the Adventurer). (Neither of these manga has been translated into English, and the 1930s-era racial caricatures in *Bōken Dankichi* make it unlikely that it ever will be published in the U.S.)

During WWII, printing supply shortages and heavy government censorship all but killed Japan's fledgling comics industry. Almost the lone bright spot of the era was the imaginative and charming artist Noboru Ōshiro, who published three full-color graphic novels for children—*Kasei Tanken* (Mars Exploration), *Kisha Ryokô* (Train Journey), and *Yukaina Tekkousho* (The Happy Steel Mill)—between 1940 and 1941. Ōshiro's books were some of the first manga to tell self-contained, book-length stories, and *Kasei Tanken* is often credited as the first science fiction manga.

In the postwar era, boys' magazines began to feature more and more comics. In some magazines, the comics sections became so popular that they gradually took over the entire magazine. Thus were the first manga magazines born. Young artists, hungry for work, rushed to fill the demand.

By far the most influential of these artists was Osamu Tezuka, who created much of the distinctive style of Japanese comics. Tezuka's first major manga, the 1947 pirate adventure *Shin Takarajima* (New Treasure Island), set the template for all future *shōnen* manga: adventure stories with cinematic action and simple, cartoony, instantly readable artwork. By the 1950s, manga had become one of the most popular forms of children's entertainment. The artists who followed in Tezuka's footsteps produced a dazzling variety of action, comedy, horror, science fiction, and fantasy manga to thrill children of all ages.

~ ~ ~ ~ ~ ~ ~ ~ ~

Section 2: Genres

Samurai and Ninja

Japan's feudal period, stretching roughly from the 12th to 19th centuries, has long provided fodder for *shōnen* manga. Mitsuteru Yokoyama's untranslated *The Silent Sword*, first published in 1955, inspired many artists to try their hands at action-adventure stories featuring samurai, ninja, and other historical heroes and villains. Yokoyama himself went on to even greater fame as the creator of the giant-robot series *Gigantor*.

Rurouni Kenshin, by Nobuhiro Watsuki, is the most popular samurai manga in the U.S. and a perennial top seller in the American manga market. *Kenshin* begins with samurai and assassin Himura Kenshin vowing to become a pacifist and make amends for all the deaths he caused. Kenshin tries to build a new life with Kaoru, a fiery young woman who runs a kendo school, but, inevitably, his past catches up to him. The manga's unusual mixture of serious historical drama with romantic comedy helped make it a hit with American audiences.

Ninja, the spies and assassins of medieval Japan, have long been popular with American audiences. By far the most successful modern ninja manga is Masashi Kishimoto's long-running series *Naruto*. In a fantasy world ruled by rival clans of ninja, Naruto, a teenage troublemaker, vows to become a master ninja and the leader of his village. A hit in Japan, *Naruto* is even more popular in the U.S., where it's the all-time best-selling manga.

Martial Arts and Fighting Tournaments

Like American superhero comics, action manga often pit characters against each other in battles between good and evil, or at least Us vs. Them. But why throw a boring punch when you can use cool-looking martial arts like karate, kung fu, or kendo? Or, better yet, why not master the secret art of *nen*, summon a supernatural Stand, or compress your cosmo to the limit for a Pegasus Rolling Crush?

Shōnen manga featuring elaborate martial arts battles grew out of more realistic manga about samurai, ninja, and martial artists. In the 1980s, *Shōnen Jump* magazine was the place to go for manga about tough guys blasting each other to pieces with improbably powerful fighting techniques—as in Tetsuo Hara's influential *Fist of the North Star*, in which the fictional *Hokuto Shinken* martial arts style makes opponents literally explode. Martial arts manga often traded DNA with psychic manga, another popular 1980s genre, producing series like *Jojo's Bizarre Adventure* by Hirohiko Araki, in which the characters fight surreal psychic battles with supernatural familiars called Stands. Meanwhile, comedy manga like Rumiko Takahashi's *Ranma 1/2* poked fun at the genre with outlandish comedy martial arts battles.

In the 1990s, as comedy and romance became more popular in *shōnen* manga, the violence in action manga was toned down and the heroes changed from musclemen to cute young teens. Video games began to influence the way action was portrayed. The enormous success of the video game, anime, and manga franchise *Pokémon*, created in 1996, introduced a new concept: tournaments in which monsters or other creatures fight on behalf of their young trainers.

Female characters became a larger presence in the formerly ultramacho world of fighting manga. CLAMP's *shōnen* manga *Angelic Layer*, for instance, focuses on girls (and a few boys) who train robotic dolls to fight in tournaments. At the same time, the classic tough-guy fighting ethos survived in manga like Nobuyuki Anzai's modern-day ninja manga *Flame of Recca*, Yoshihiro Togashi's supernatural martial arts manga *YuYu Hakusho*, and, of course, Akira Toriyama's *Dragon Ball*.

During its massively popular 1996–2004 run, Kazuki Takahashi's *Yu-Gi-Oh!* proved that a battle manga doesn't need to involve physical fights. Initially an episodic manga featuring games and puzzles, *Yu-Gi-Oh!* tapped an unexpected vein of popularity when it introduced a collectible card game—a thinly disguised version of *Magic: The Gathering*. The card game tournaments were such a hit with readers that they soon dominated the manga.

Today, anything can turn into a martial arts battle. Shinji Saijyo's *Iron Wok Jan* depicts cooking competitions as intense as any confrontation in *Fist of the North Star*. Takashi Hashiguchi's *Yakitate!! Japan*, about a boy competing to bake the greatest loaf of bread in Japan, satirizes the melodrama and escalating power levels of fighting manga. (In one chapter, a character bakes bread so delicious that anyone who eats it *dies of pleasure*.) In *shōnen* manga, whether you're living in a postapocalyptic wasteland or just whipping up dinner, be prepared for a fight.

Horror

Kids love a good scare, but the first manga magazines were reluctant to run horror for fear that it would be seen as a bad influence on children. (The American comics world dealt with similar concerns in the 1950s, when horror comics like *Tales from the Crypt* sparked an anticomics backlash.) Instead of being serialized in magazines, early horror manga was usually published in cheap paperback books designed for manga rental stores.

Soon, however, even respectable publishers began to see the appeal of spooky—but not too scary—manga featuring sympathetic monsters and ghosts. Shigeru Mizuki's *GeGeGe no Kitarō*, which ran from 1959 to 1969 in *Weekly Shōnen Magazine*, enthralled children with the adventures of a one-eyed boy who lives in a graveyard inhabited by *yokai*, a catchall term for supernatural monsters and spirits.

As time went on, however, horror manga grew more graphic and frightening. Kazuo Umezu, who rose to prominence in the 1960s and 1970s, is widely acknowledged as the master of manga horror. Looking at his work now, it's amazing that so much of it ran in mainstream *shōnen* or *shōjo* magazines rather than more adult formats. The same goes for the equally influential Go Nagai, whose graphically violent *Devilman* ran in *Weekly Shōnen Magazine*. The work of Hideshi Hino combined cute, cartoonish characters with graphically horrific imagery in works like *Hell Baby* and *Panorama of Hell*.

Today, *shōnen* horror manga tends to be less scary and is often crossed with action and/or comedy, producing lighter alternatives to the pure horror found in manga for older audiences. Many *shōnen* manga incorporate supernatural elements like monsters, vengeful spirits, or black magic to give the action a spooky edge. The countless examples include Yellow Tanabe's *Kekkaishi*, in which two high-schoolers moonlight as hunters of the evil spirits that haunt their school grounds; Ryohgo Narita and Akiyo Satorigi's *Durarara!!*, in which a motorcycle-riding Irish ghost haunts a Japanese neighborhood; and CLAMP's *Gate 7*, in which magical warriors in modern-day Kyoto fight traditional Japanese spirits.

In recent years, manga featuring *shinigami*—death spirits comparable to the Western concept of the Grim Reaper—have become popular. These include Tite Kubo's *Bleach*, about a teenage boy who becomes a Soul Reaper after a brush with death; Yoshihiro Togashi's *YuYu Hakusho*, in which a juvenile delinquent gets a second chance as a fighting ghost; *Boogiepop Phantom*, in which a city is haunted by a bizarre but benevolent *shinigami* called Boogiepop; and, of course, the enormously popular *Death Note*.

Manga with gothic themes and art styles are currently trendy. Popular goth-themed *shōnen* manga include Yana Toboso's *Black Butler*, about a demonic butler who is bound by a supernatural contract to serve a mortal boy, and Katsura Hoshino's *D. Gray-man*, set in a version of Victorian England where exorcists fight demonic creatures. Zombies are also a popular subject, as in Daisuke Satō and Shōji Satō's *Highschool of the Dead*.

Sports

Name any contest, and there's a manga about it. Tennis? Takeshi Konomi's *Prince of Tennis*. Inline skating? Oh! Great's *Air Gear*. Car racing? Noboru Mitsusawa's *Initial D*. Board games? Yumi Hotta and Takeshi Obata's *Hikaru no Go*. Collectible card games? Kazuki Takahashi's blockbuster *Yu-Gi-Oh!* and its countless imitators. And manga dealing with video games, starting with 1980s arcade-game manga like the untranslated *Game Center Arashi*, are too numerous to list.

In Japan, as in the U.S., baseball is the most beloved of sports. Surprisingly, although there are dozens of baseball-themed *shōnen* manga, most have not been translated into English. One of the rare exceptions is *Cross Game* by Mitsuru Adachi, an artist famous in Japan for mixing sports drama with warm-hearted romantic comedy.

In the early 1990s, Takehiko Inoue almost single-handedly popularized basketball in Japan with his hit series *Slam Dunk*. More recently, Inoue has drawn *Buzzer Beater*, a basketball webcomic produced in collaboration with ESPN, and *Real*, a *seinen* manga about wheelchair basketball. Other basketball manga include Yuriko Nishiyama's *Harlem Beat* and the untranslated *Dear Boys*, by Hiroki Yagami.

The "sports entertainment" of pro wrestling is as robust in Japan as it is in the U.S., and few manga are as iconic in Japan as the 1980s pro wrestling comedy *Kinnikuman* (Muscleman), by the two-man team Yudetamago. *Kinnikuman* remains untranslated in English, but its raunchy 2000s sequel, *Ultimate Muscle*, is available in translation.

The classic soccer manga, Takahashi Yoichi's *Captain Tsubasa*, has yet to be translated into English, but soccer is represented in translation with Daisuke Higuchi's more recent series *Whistle!* Meanwhile, American-style football features in Riichirô Inagaki and Yusuke Murata's slapstick comedy *Eyeshield 21*.

Science Fiction and Fantasy

In the late 1940s, Osamu Tezuka followed his first hit manga, *New Treasure Island*, with his "science fiction trilogy," three manga loosely inspired by the posters for sci-fi movies. *Lost World, Metropolis,* and *Nextworld* (inspired by the movie *Things to Come*) incorporated ideas from movies and pulp science fiction, especially the stories of Isaac Asimov. In 1952, Tezuka launched *Tetsuwan Atom* (Mighty Atom), known in the U.S. as *Astro Boy*, setting the tone for decades of science fiction manga to follow.

From Tezuka onward, *shōnen* manga magazines have featured plenty of series with science fiction and fantasy themes. Starting in the mid-1980s, science fiction and fantasy began to overtake more realistic genres like samurai, martial arts, and sports manga in popularity. Much of this change can be attributed to the massive success of two key *Shōnen Jump* manga. Masami Kurumada's *Saint Seiya*, published in the U.S. as *Knights of the Zodiac*, transplanted the intense action and torturous training sequences of classic sports manga to a fantasy setting, spinning a tale about five warriors who defend the goddess Athena with powers based on the Western zodiac. Meanwhile, Akira Toriyama's *Dragon Ball*, a lighthearted fantasy which gradually transforms into a science-fiction superhero story, broke all manga sales records.

Today, popular science fiction and fantasy manga run the gamut from the Harry Potter–inspired comedy *Negima!* to the alchemy-based *Fullmetal Alchemist* and *Buso Renkin* to the alternate-universe fantasy *Tsubasa: Reservoir Chronicle* to *Naruto*, which updates the traditional ninja manga by setting it in a richly drawn fantasy world.

Mecha

"Mecha" refers to robots, but especially to the giant robots that are almost synonymous with Japanese pop culture. The giant-robot genre began with Mitsuteru Yokoyama's 1956 manga *Tetsujin 28-Go*, known in the U.S. as *Gigantor*. Although the *Gigantor* manga has never been translated into English, the TV anime adaptation was well known to American children growing up in the 1960s.

In 1972, Go Nagai's *Mazinger Z*, also known in the U.S. as *Tranzor Z*, established many of the staples of mecha manga, especially the idea of a pilot controlling the robot from inside its head. Nagai's concept of "a robot that you could drive" inspired a host of other manga and anime.

The sprawling, long-running *Gundam* franchise began as an anime series in 1979 and has since spawned a seemingly endless array of spinoffs, including multiple manga. Like many popular mecha series, *Gundam* features a team of robot pilots, rather than a lone hero, and makes the characters' relationships a key part of the story. Although a *shōnen* series, *Gundam* has a large female fan following, thanks in part to the 1990s series *Gundam Wing*, featuring a team of handsome and appealingly written young pilots.

In the 1990s, mecha went through a dark reworking with the blockbuster anime series *Neon Genesis Evangelion*, created by Hideaki Anno, in which young mecha pilots deal with both internal traumas and monstrous invaders in a postapocalyptic Japan. The *Evangelion* manga adaptation by Yoshiyuki Sadamoto, the character designer for the anime, began in 1994, ten months before the anime premiered on television, and is still running over fifteen years after the end of the original anime.

Romantic Comedy

Even in the high-octane world of *shōnen* manga, romance, especially romantic comedy, is popular. *Shōnen* romance often involves a relationship between an average guy and a remarkable dream girl (sometimes with magical or sci-fi powers), or else a "harem" of appealing potential love interests.

Almost all modern *shōnen* romantic comedies stem from the work of Rumiko Takahashi. Takahashi's *Urusei Yatsura*, a 1970s–1980s slapstick comedy featuring a dimwitted horndog "hero," a bikini-clad alien demon girl who fries her beloved with lightning bolts, and an ever-expanding cast of sexy super-powered women and wacky sidekicks, created the template for both "magical girlfriend" and "harem" manga. It also popularized romantic comedies with supernatural or science fiction elements. Takahashi's next *shōnen* manga, *Ranma 1/2*, offered a similar blend of romance, slapstick comedy, and magic.

Many popular *shōnen* manga of the 1980s and 1990s followed the trail blazed by Takahashi, usually with more romance and less comedy. Masakazu Katsura's *Video Girl Ai*, the dream girl comes out of an enchanted videotape. Katsura has said that he only added the fantasy premise to *Video Girl Ai* so it would sell, and his more recent romance manga, *I"s*, is set at an ordinary high school.

Nowadays, romance manga are often more down to earth. But there's still room for outrageous comedy, as in bizarre manga like Kazurou Inoue's *Midori Days*, in which a miniature girl sprouts from the hero's right arm (yes, his right hand literally is his girlfriend) or Yasuhiro Kanō's *Pretty Face*, whose unfortunate hero is maimed in an accident and rescued by an insane plastic surgeon who reconstructs him into an exact copy of the girl he loves. Manga based on "dating sim" relationship video games or on so-called "light novels" have also become common.

Over time, *shōnen* romance has grown heavier on "fanservice" cheesecake material. Ken Akamatsu, who began his professional career in the 1990s, often pushes the boundaries of nudity and raunchy humor in manga like *Negima!* and *Love Hina*. On the opposite end of titillation levels, *moe* manga featuring chaste romances between innocent, young-looking characters have also gained in popularity.

~ ~ ~ ~ ~ ~ ~ ~ ~ ~

Section 3: Special Issues

Audience and Age Divisions

In Japan, most manga is serialized in magazines before being collected into graphic-novel-style paperbacks, or *tankoubon*. In recent years, the magazines have increasingly become "loss leaders" that hook readers so they'll later buy the *tankoubon* collections. Although manga magazines exist for every conceivable niche market, *shōnen* manga magazines—aimed broadly at boys eighteen and under—are the biggest sellers.

Shōnen Jump, the flagship magazine of publisher Shueisha, is consistently the best-selling manga magazine in Japan. During its high point in the 1990s, when it serialized Akira Toriyama's megahit *Dragon Ball*, *Shōnen Jump* sold over six million copies a week. Not only is it popular with boys, but it frequently tops polls of girls' favorite manga magazines, beating out the magazines aimed at a female audience. *Jump*'s chief rivals, *Weekly Shōnen Magazine* (published by Kodansha) and *Shōnen Sunday* (published by Shogakukan), are also top sellers with their own stables of hits.

Of the three major *shōnen* magazines, *Shōnen Jump* has a reputation for action-oriented, mostly preteen-friendly adventure manga based on a single reliable formula. Early in the magazine's history, the editors ran a survey asking their young readers for three words: the thing that warmed their hearts the most, the thing they felt was most important, and the thing that made them happiest. The answers: *yūjō* (friendship), *doryoku* (effort), and *shōri* (victory). Ever since, nearly every manga published in *Shōnen Jump* has incorporated these three core values. The typical *Jump* manga features optimistic young heroes working hard to achieve victory, discovering the power of friendship along the way.

Compared to *Shōnen Jump,* competitor *Shōnen Sunday* tends to publish less action-oriented fare and more comedy and romance, often with cute, polished, animation-friendly artwork. Rumiko Takahashi's hit manga *Urusei Yatsura, Ranma 1/2,* and *Inuyasha* all ran in *Sunday*, and her light, witty style remains the magazine's touchstone. In Japan, the most popular current *Shōnen Sunday* manga is Gosho Aoyama's long-running mystery series *Case Closed,* about a detective who continues to solve crimes after a strange formula turns him into a little boy.

The third major *shōnen* magazine, *Weekly Shōnen Magazine,* leans toward more down-to-earth manga, often with realistic artwork and tough-guy loner heroes. Whereas both *Jump* and *Sunday* cater happily to the *otaku* (geek) audience with plenty of sci-fi and fantasy stories, *Weekly Shōnen* is the place to go for manga set in the real world (or at least a cool, idealized version of the real world), although it's also published popular fantasy manga like Ken Akamatsu's *Negima!* and CLAMP's *Tsubasa: Reservoir Chronicle.*

All three magazines are aimed at an audience of roughly junior-high-age boys, sometimes skewing a little older or a little younger. Smaller *shōnen* magazines often focus on different age groups. Magazines for elementary schoolers include *Corocoro Comic, Comic Bombom,* and the Tentomushi Comics imprint, which publishes a family of magazines identified by grade level: *Shogaku Ichinensei* (First Grade), *Shogaku Ninensei* (Second Grade), and so on. Manga based on kiddie media franchises like *Pokémon* are popular with this age group.

Magazines skewed toward older teens include *Shōnen Sirius, Shōnen Champion,* and *Shōnen Rival. Shōnen* manga for older readers tends to feature more realistic artwork, more violent action, and, of course, more sexy pinup art.

Fanservice

Shōnen manga, especially those skewed toward older boys, often feature a fair amount of cheesecake, or "fanservice." Skimpy outfits, flashes of underwear (especially panties), suggestive poses, and other forms of T&A are common in romance and comedy manga, but also sometimes in action series. Outright nudity is usually, though not always, covered. Even the raciest *shōnen* manga, however, is unlikely to feature actual sex between characters. (By contrast, *shōjo* manga aimed at older girls do sometimes include discreetly drawn sex scenes.)

The level and type of sexual content largely depends on the manga's intended audience. Manga that originally appeared in *Shōnen Jump* magazine, for example, often go easy on the T&A, in part because *Shōnen Jump* has a large female audience. *Shōnen Jump* manga may even include fanservice for female readers in the form of sexy male characters and/or homoerotic tension between the heroes. In the first chapter of *Naruto,* for example, Naruto and his rival Sasuke accidentally kiss, while the handsome male leads of *Death Note* spend several chapters handcuffed together.

Some *shōnen* manga, especially those aimed at older readers, exist primarily to deliver fanservice. The magazine *Shōnen Champion,* which ran Go Nagai's untranslated T&A action comedy *Cutie Honey* in the 1970s, has a reputation for outrageous, over-the-top manga like Seiji Matsuyama's infamous *Eiken,* with its cast of enormous-breasted girls forever falling into pornographic-looking poses, and Morishige's *Hanaukyo Maid Team,* part of the currently popular subgenre of manga featuring girls in maid outfits.

~ ~ ~ ~ ~ ~ ~ ~ ~

Section 4: Notable Artists

Osamu Tezuka

Osamu Tezuka, the "God of Manga," is revered as the inventor of the distinctive stylistic elements of manga: big-eyed, iconic characters, detailed backgrounds, and an impressionistic approach to storytelling designed to make the reader feel the action and emotion.

Tezuka started drawing manga in his early twenties while attending medical school, and his work soon became so successful that he gave up on his medical career (he reportedly hated the sight of blood) to become a full-time artist. His first book-length manga, *New Treasure Island*, was a surprise bestseller, and he followed it with a flood of dynamic, endlessly inventive manga that awed generations of children.

Whereas other manga artists at the time drew in styles influenced by American newspaper comics, Tezuka took his cue from Disney animation and European films, trying to create a sense of motion and action on the page. As he explained in his autobiography, "I experimented with close-ups and different angles, and instead of using only one frame for an action scene or the climax (as was customary), I made a point of depicting a movement or facial expression with many frames, even many pages."

Over the course of his career, Tezuka worked in every conceivable genre. But few of his works are as beloved as his popular *shōnen* manga series, including *Astro Boy, Kimba the White Lion,* the medical action drama *Black Jack*, the religious history *Buddha,* and the unfinished samurai adventure *Dororo.*

Kazuo Umezu

In Japan, horror artist Kazuo Umezu is known not only as a legendary manga pioneer, but as one of the country's most beloved eccentrics. "Umezz" can often be seen on the streets and subways of Tokyo in his signature permed hair and childlike red-and-white-striped shirt; his house is painted in red and white stripes to match.

Born in 1936, Umezu began his manga career as a teenager, and his stiff but arresting artwork attracted the admiration of Osamu Tezuka himself. Much of Umezu's early work was published in *shōjo* manga magazines, but he also drew horror manga for manga rental stores, a less respectable venue than magazines. As Umezu developed an interest in the fledgling genre of *gekiga*, alternative comics for adults, he started incorporating surreal, psychological horror into his work.

In 1972, Umezu began the *shōnen* manga widely considered his masterpiece, the postapocalyptic horror saga *The Drifting Classroom*. An ordinary elementary school is mysteriously teleported to a barren wasteland populated by unearthly monsters; as the adults in the school give up or lose their minds, the children are forced to fight to survive. Grim, violent, and filled with bizarre, dreamlike imagery, *The Drifting Classroom* is almost certainly the scariest manga ever to run in the pages of the usually sedate *Shōnen Sunday* magazine.

Other classic Umezu manga available in English include *Cat-Eyed Boy* and the short story anthology *Scary Book*. In recent years, he's drawn graphic horror manga like the untranslated *Fourteen* for *seinen* magazines. But Umezu isn't just a horror artist; he's also the creator of the untranslated kiddie comedy *Makoto-chan*. Asked about the difference between horror and comedy, Umezu responded, "If you're doing the chasing, it's a gag manga. If you're being chased, it's horror."

Rumiko Takahashi

At one time, Rumiko Takahashi was rumored to be the wealthiest woman in Japan outside the royal family. One of the most consistently successful manga artists, and one of a handful of women to make it big in *shōnen* manga, Takahashi has produced a steady stream of hits for over 30 years. Her first series, *Urusei Yatsura* (roughly translatable as "Those Obnoxious Aliens"), a sci-fi comedy about hapless teenager Ataru's relationship with the sexy but volatile alien demon girl Lum, was an instant success with the readers of *Shōnen Sunday* magazine. Takahashi followed *Urusei Yatsura* with *Maison Ikkoku*, a *seinen* romantic comedy that many consider her best work, then *Ranma 1/2*, a raucous *shōnen* comedy about a tough-guy martial artist who turns into a girl when he gets wet.

In 1996, Takahashi began her longest work to date, *Inuyasha*, a darker, less comedic manga in which a teenage girl travels back in time to ancient Japan where she meets the half-demon warrior Inuyasha. *Inuyasha* was enormously popular in both Japan and the U.S. Takahashi's current series, *Rin-Ne*, follows a girl who can see ghosts and a boy descended from *shinigami* (death spirits) as they help restless ghosts.

Takahashi's work mixes fantasy, action, romance, and slapstick comedy into an energetic blend that appeals to a wide range of readers. Her artwork, with big-eyed, friendly characters drawn in such a cheerful style that even the fanservice looks wholesome, has equally broad appeal. Her work was some of the first manga to catch on in the U.S., winning both male and female fans, and continues to be popular to this day.

Akira Toriyama

Arguably the most influential *shōnen* artist of the 1980s and 1990s, Akira Toriyama helped turn *Shōnen Jump* magazine into a powerhouse. Toriyama's beloved 1980s series *Dr. Slump* follows a hyperactive little robot girl named Arale and her bumbling creator around the whimsical town of Penguin Village. With its rollicking mix of visual gags, wordplay, pop-culture references, and bathroom humor, all drawn in a charming but detailed style showing off Toriyama's exceptional draftsmanship, *Dr. Slump* delighted a generation of Japanese children.

But *Dr. Slump* was soon overshadowed by the stratospheric success of Toriyama's next series, *Dragon Ball,* which ran for 11 years (1984–1995) during what fans call "the Golden Age of *Jump.*" *Dragon Ball* starts as a comic fantasy riffing on the classical Chinese story of the Monkey King, represented in the manga by a superstrong, monkey-tailed little boy named Goku. As the manga progresses, however, the characters get older and the plot more serious and action oriented, until it becomes a superhero epic with muscular heroes and villains deploying planet-flattening martial arts. This change in tone may be one of the reasons for *Dragon Ball*'s staggering success, both in Japan and abroad: it grows up with its readers, starting as a manga for children and ending as a manga for teenagers. The first and second halves of the series are so different that, in the U.S., they are published as two separate titles, *Dragon Ball* and *Dragon Ball Z.*

Because *Dragon Ball* was so massively successful, publisher Shueisha pushed Toriyama to keep drawing it long past the point at which he would have preferred to quit. Since then, he has restricted himself to short manga of one volume or less, and has mostly returned to the childlike art style of *Dr. Slump*. Toriyama's more recent manga include *Cowa!*, about a mischievous half-vampire, half-werekoala living in a monster village, and *Sand Land*, a *Mad Max*–like adventure set in a postapocalyptic desert world.

Ken Akamatsu

Ken Akamatsu started his manga career as a fan artist, winning a following for his illustrations while he was still in college. He advanced to a professional career almost immediately after graduation, drawing one-shots and short series before finding a hit with *A.I. Love You*, a sci-fi romantic comedy about a computer programmer whose AI comes to life as a sexy girl.

Akamatsu followed *A.I. Love You* with the enormously popular *Love Hina*. Following a promise to a childhood friend, aspiring college student Keitaro moves into a dorm while cramming for the Tokyo University exams, only to be distracted by the many sexy girls sharing the building with him. Just as the plot of *A.I. Love You* borrows heavily from earlier romantic comedy manga like *Oh My Goddess!* and *Video Girl Ai* (as well as the John Hughes movie *Weird Science*), *Love Hina* owes an enormous debt to Rumiko Takahashi's *seinen* romantic comedy *Maison Ikkoku*, also about an aspiring college student trying to study in a raucous apartment building.

What Akamatsu brought to the standard *shōnen* romantic comedy formula was a raunchy sense of humor and a lot of cheesecake. Reviewing *Love Hina* for *Manga: The Complete Guide,* Jason Thompson wrote, "It's less about merely flashing the reader with T&A and more about cramming as many sex jokes as possible into each chapter . . . It's a love comedy with the emphasis on *comedy*." The influence of Rumiko Takahashi also shows in Akamatsu's art, which is cute, expressive, and filled with over-the-top comedy violence.

After *Love Hina*, Akamatsu turned his fanboy sensors to another popular franchise and created *Negima!*, a manga about a bespectacled boy wizard at a boarding school. Although fans sometimes refer to *Negima!* as "Love Hogwarts," the premise is somewhat different: Negi the wizard is only ten years old, he's a precocious teacher rather than a student . . . and, inevitably, all his students are cute girls. More recently, Akamatsu created the sci-fi anime and manga series *Mao-chan*, a wacky comedy about cute little girls who are recruited to fight equally cute aliens.

Masashi Kishimoto

Masashi Kishimoto's career path is typical of *shōnen* manga artists, but few have followed it so successfully. Like many aspiring manga creators, Kishimoto enrolled in an art college after high school. While still at college, he began submitting short manga to *shōnen* magazines. His first story, "Karakuri," won *Shōnen Jump*'s monthly "Hop Step" award and attracted the attention of editors. His next published story, "Naruto," appeared a year later. Both stories were picked up by publisher Shueisha and became weekly series in *Shōnen Jump*, but *Karakuri* was quickly canceled. *Naruto*, however, survived to become one of the most popular manga of the 2000s.

From the beginning of his career, Kishimoto was interested in creating a manga based on historical Japan, a genre not often represented in *Shōnen Jump*. *Naruto* involves ninjas and Japanese mythology, but the setting is unique, a fantasy vision of Japan where the medieval and modern rub shoulders and ninjas wear contemporary-looking goggles and windbreakers. (The early short-story version even included motorcycles.) Naruto, the class clown of his village's ninja school, vows to hone his underused talents and become the village's *hokage,* or leader. His classmates have their own goals, and as the manga continues it becomes a sprawling epic of battling ninja clans.

Still ongoing, *Naruto* is currently 60 volumes long. It's become one of the top-selling manga of all time in Japan, but it's been even more successful with international readers. In the U.S., *Naruto* is the all-time bestselling manga and has a massive fan following. In 2006, nearly one in every ten manga sold in the U.S. was a volume of *Naruto*.

Eiichiro Oda

Naruto may be the most popular manga in the U.S., but in Japan that honor belongs to Eiichiro Oda's *One Piece*, which also runs in *Shōnen Jump* magazine. With over 260 million volumes sold in Japan, it's the best-selling manga in Japanese history.

In the U.S., Oda's work has been slower to catch on, although it has a growing and loyal fan following. Perhaps it's too offbeat for many American fans. In a world of vast oceans and exotic islands, aspiring pirate Monkey D. Luffy sets out with a rowboat and a dream, eager to form his own pirate crew. Thanks to a magic fruit he ate as a boy, Luffy has the power to stretch like rubber, which he employs in ingenious fighting techniques. But he's not the only superpowered pirate out there, and as Luffy and his friends advance in the world of piracy they encounter bigger, badder, and weirder rivals.

Oda is strongly influenced by *Dragon Ball* creator Akira Toriyama; when asked in an interview for his three favorite manga, he answered, "Everything by Akira Toriyama." Oda's art has Toriyama's energy and cartoony charm, but over the course of *One Piece* he's developed his own unmistakable style, designing characters and settings so wildly abstracted they resemble the psychedelic art of Peter Max or the movie *Yellow Submarine*.

Oda started submitting manga to publishers as a teenager and came in second for the prestigious Tezuka Award at the age of 17. This got him a job as an art assistant for *Shōnen Jump*. Like many manga artists, Oda learned his craft as an assistant to established artists—including, in his case, *Rurouni Kenshin* creator Nobuhiro Watsuki. While assisting Watsuki, he drew short pirate manga, one of which, "Romance Dawn," was published in *Jump*. Reworked into an ongoing story, "Romance Dawn" became *One Piece*, the pirate manga that conquered Japan.

Yoshihiro Togashi

In one sense, Yoshihiro Togashi's energetic, if unevenly drawn, action epics are the quintessential *shōnen* manga. In another sense, they're like nothing else. Like many manga artists, Togashi puts his own mark on well-worn genres with outlandish, aggressively weird characters and concepts.

After drawing several romance and comedy manga, Togashi finally hit it big in 1990 with *YuYu Hakusho* (roughly translatable as "The Ghost Files"), about a teen delinquent who dies heroically and is granted the opportunity to earn his way back to the world of the living as an "underworld detective." Over the course of the series, *YuYu Hakusho* changes from a supernatural crime story to a tournament-style fighting manga in which characters battle with otherworldly martial arts. In an unusual move, Togashi ended *YuYu Hakusho* while the series was still at the height of its popularity.

In 1998, Togashi began his next major series, *Hunter X Hunter* (the "X" is silent), which is even harder to categorize. Set in a fantasy world full of strange societies and complex rules, *Hunter X Hunter* begins as a tournament manga in which the young hero Gon competes—in physical battles, but also in card games, puzzles, and other contests—for the right to become one of the Hunters, an elite group of adventurers. Once Gon and his friends attain the rank of Hunter, Togashi uses the premise to explore every conceivable genre of *shōnen* manga, from martial arts to video games to apocalyptic science fiction.

Whereas most manga running in magazines follow a scrupulous weekly or monthly schedule, *Hunter X Hunter* updates slowly and sporadically. Togashi has taken numerous hiatuses from drawing, sometimes due to health problems, and the art in *Hunter X Hunter* often looks sketchy and rushed. This hasn't affected the popularity of the series, which has an enthusiastic cult following in both Japan and the U.S.

Hiromu Arakawa

A female artist working openly under a male pen name (her real name is Hiromi), Arakawa started her career as a manga artist's assistant and launched her first series, the untranslated *Stray Dog*, in 1999. But it wasn't until her third series, *Fullmetal Alchemist*, that she emerged as one of the new millennium's rising talents in *shōnen* manga.

Fullmetal Alchemist takes place in a fantasy world reminiscent of Enlightenment-era Europe where alchemy is real and is treated as a scientific discipline. Two brothers, Edward and Alphonse Elric, wander the world searching for a cure for an alchemical accident that disabled them. Edward lost an arm and a leg, while

Alphonse lost his entire body and exists as a soul inhabiting a suit of armor. As the Elrics battle the Homunculi, a group of alchemical beings named after the Seven Deadly Sins, they uncover disturbing revelations about their society. The manga's unusual setting and clean, detailed art made it an instant hit and won Arakawa the Tezuka Cultural Prize for "New Artist." It's one of the most popular manga in the U.S.

In addition to *Fullmetal Alchemist*, Arakawa's manga *Hero Tales*, a Chinese martial-arts drama written by Huang Jim Zhou, is available in English translation. Her current, untranslated series *Silver Spoon*, about a teenager who enrolls in an agricultural vocational school because he mistakenly thinks it will be easier than a standard high school, was inspired partly by her experiences growing up on her family's dairy farm.

Tsugumi Ohba and Takeshi Obata

It looks like an ordinary notebook—but write someone's name in it, and that person will die. With this grim premise, writer Tsugumi Ohba and artist Takeshi Obata begin *Death Note*, one of the most macabre but enthralling manga ever to darken the pages of the normally sunny magazine *Shōnen Jump*. The notebook belongs to a *shinigami* (death spirit) who drops it in the mortal world. There, it's discovered by Light Yagami, a brilliant teenager who thinks he can use the notebook for good by eliminating criminals under the code name "Kira," but quickly becomes a megalomaniac in the process. L, an equally brilliant and unhinged young detective, sets out to stop the mysterious killer, and the two lock wits in complex set pieces of intellectual one-upmanship.

Death Note was a massive hit with teens in Japan and abroad, despite—or perhaps because of—adult concerns over its ghoulish premise. Authorities in parts of China banned the manga, explaining that horror "misleads innocent children and distorts their mind and spirit." In many schools worldwide, including in the U.S., students were suspended, expelled, and even arrested for creating homemade "Death Notes" with the names of fellow students. Perhaps these fears were not entirely unfounded; in 2007, a corpse was discovered in Belgium alongside two notes reading "I am Kira" in Latin. The "Manga Murder" case has yet to be solved.

Before *Death Note*, artist Takeshi Obata drew the unlikely hit *Hikaru no Go*, written by Yumi Hotta, about a boy who is trained in the traditional board game Go by a medieval ghost. Obata's striking artwork, with its detailed backgrounds, cinematic camera angles, and dramatically lit splashes of black and white, leant intensity to potentially static scenes of characters playing board games, and it likewise helped raise the visual tension in the talky, brainy *Death Note*. The photorealism of Obata's artwork was unusual for *shōnen* manga when *Death Note* started, but, since the manga's 2003–2006 run, it's inspired a host of imitators.

Writer Tsugumi Ohba is an enigma. "He" is known to write under a pen name, and his/her identity is a closely guarded secret. After *Death Note*, Ohba and Obata teamed up again for *Bakuman*, about two teenage boys who join forces to make it as manga creators. Like *Death Note, Bakuman* is an unusually wordy and cerebral manga, balancing the typical *Shōnen Jump* tone of big-hearted competitive spirit with an exhaustively described, sometimes cynical insider's look at the modern manga industry.

Chapter 3

Shōjo Manga

by Sean Gaffney

Section 1: History

Like its counterpart for boys, *shōjo* manga is rooted in the comic strips that ran in girls' magazines from the 1910s until World War II. Though not as sophisticated as today's manga, these strips provided readers with entertaining stories and escapism, including the "girl as action hero" type of epic that many fans credit Osamu Tezuka with pioneering in *Princess Knight*. A good twenty years before Tezuka, however, artist Katsuji Matsumoto was creating illustrations and short manga stories for the magazine *Shôjo Gaho* (Girls Illustrated), including the Robin Hoodesque *Mysterious Clover* and the humorously weird *Kurukuru Kurumi-chan*.

With the manga industry's resurgence after World War II, *Anmitsu Hime* was a big hit, following the standard prewar short comic situations template. Here is where Tezuka comes in. *Princess Knight* was a long-form adventure featuring action, romance, and psychological issues, taking *shōjo* to a deeper, more meaningful place than it had ever gone before. Indeed, before the 1950s, romance was almost unheard of in *shōjo* manga, whose heroines were typically the same age as their preteen readers. The 1950s also saw the introduction of two of the most prominent *shōjo* magazines, Kodansha's *Nakayoshi* and Shueisha's *Ribon*, which both continue to this day.

The first female creator to really show Japan the future of *shōjo* manga was Yoshiko Nishitani, who wrote for Shueisha's *Margaret* magazine. Nishitani's *Mary Lou* is credited with being one of the first "school romance" stories, which—if you look at the shelves of any bookstore with manga on it today—form a large percentage of current manga plots. Her stories also were written for young teenagers from 13 to

15 years old, rather than little girls. The "manga boom" of the late 1960s broadened *shōjo* even further. This period's influx of female creators (including the Year 24 Group, described on page 55) was not content to focus on children's stories, or even school romance. They wrote fantasy and science fiction, horror, realistic family and school situations, and of course one of the biggest new trends—romance between two young men written specifically for women, known now as *yaoi* or boys' love (BL).

As readers grew up, the target age for *shōjo* magazines continued to rise, even as many readers graduated to *josei* comics meant for young women. Some magazines—the most prominent being Shogakukan's *Shōjo Comic*—now publish romance manga with sexual situations that would have been unheard of even as late as the early 1980s.

Today, *shōjo* magazines are published for a variety of age demographics. *Ribon* and *Nakayoshi* (along with Shogakukan's *Ciao*, which began in 1977) still publish stories predominantly for girls aged 8–12, while *shōjo* powerhouse Hakusensha has cornered the teenage market with *Hana to Yume* and *LaLa*. There are magazines with a fantasy bent (Shinshokan's *Wings*), magazines for female *otaku* (Kadokawa Shoten's *Asuka*), and magazines that straddle the line between teens and young adults, with stories that may be spicy but also emotionally complex (Shueisha's *Cookie*, Hakusensha's *Melody*). Despite a decrease in manga sales that began in 1995, *shōjo* manga still remains a vibrant and creative genre, and its creators—in stark contrast to 60 years ago—are now almost entirely women.

~ ~ ~ ~ ~ ~ ~ ~ ~

Section 2: Genres

Romantic Comedy

First off, it needs to be said that 95% of all *shōjo* manga, no matter the genre, will be dealing with romance in some way. It's simply the nature of what *shōjo* publishers look for. Somewhere in the manga, there has to be a love story. Of course, not all *shōjo* manga are *just* love stories, but many are, and a great many of these fall into the category of "romantic comedy." *Shōjo* romantic comedy typically involves teenagers who meet under amusing circumstances in a school setting, such as in series like *Ouran High School Host Club*, *Otomen*, *Dengeki Daisy*, or *Love*Com*. Romantic comedy is an incredibly popular genre in North America, with volumes consistently ranking in the *New York Times* bestseller charts. This is not to say that there aren't dramatic or heartfelt moments in these titles, but they tend to be sweet and amusing first and foremost. There are various types of romantic couples that feature prominently in these books—for example, the overly perky, naive girl and the sullen young man who just wants to be left alone. Some titles flip this dynamic around by featuring a cool, reserved heroine who finds herself falling for a happy, overly enthusiastic guy. These romantic couplings will be familiar to readers of Western romance fiction, and the situations they find themselves in are also intended to resonate with teenaged readers, Japanese or otherwise. Things like communication mishaps, jealous rivals, school festivals, and first kisses are common plot points in *shōjo* romantic comedy.

Most of the romantic comedies licensed for publication in North America rarely progress beyond kissing, though there are exceptions. Sometimes there's a darker undertone, whether it's meant to be scary or sexy. For the most part, however, readers are intended to root for these cute kids to get together and support them once they do.

Romantic Drama

It could be argued that dramatic *shōjo* romances fare even better in North America than the comedic ones. Romantic dramas such as *Black Bird* and *Kimi ni Todoke* are consistent bestsellers. Much as *shōjo* romantic comedy can have serious and dramatic elements, *shōjo* romantic drama is not entirely angst and worry. However, the romantic drama tends to have an introspective, melancholy tone to it. These stories often feature heroines who are dealing with issues of self-confidence or school bullying, which may occur both before and after any romance that's involved.

Likewise, just because the boy and girl get together does not mean that everything is going to be happily ever after. More often than in *shōnen* romance, *shōjo* romance will continue on past the first blush of love, which is invariably followed by a teeming pit of doubts and fears. Titles such as *We Were There* or *Sand Chronicles* set up an obvious pairing, then put their leads through the wringer in much the same style as the best Western romance novels.

Dramatic *shōjo* heroines are often deceptively stoic. They may wear a cheerful mask that hides their many worries and fears. (Tohru Honda from *Fruits Basket* is a good example.) Some are simply introverts—uncomfortable and embarrassed by attention, yet constantly thrust into the limelight. One controversial yet highly popular subgenre of *shōjo* romantic drama pairs an introverted and easily embarrassed girl with a manipulative, sexy, standoffish guy, who may be protective and loving one moment and abusive and unfathomable the next.

The thrill in these manga is the same as in soap opera—desperation to find out what comes next. Most dramatic *shōjo* titles end each chapter with a cliffhanger. Readers root for the heroine to gain more self-confidence and maturity and for her newfound love to become nicer and less selfish. Often the latter comes more easily than the former. Heroines in this genre may be unfairly thought of as doormats, but in the best of these manga, the story wraps up with a truly satisfying conclusion. For the best examples of this, look to Mayu Shinjo's *Sensual Phrase* and Miki Aihara's *Hot Gimmick*.

Magical Girl

This is the genre that most people think of first when they think about *shōjo* manga—a young girl in a frilly costume fighting evil with her magical wand. Actually, the "fighting evil" part is fairly recent. The first popular magical-girl stories were more about a young girl's transformation into something different—more alluring, usually older—and how the need to keep this secret impacted the heroine's life. Idol singers, due to their fame and celebrity, were popular choices for the young magical girl. In addition, sometimes the magical girl also helped to fight crime, but usually the police wanted to catch her as well—in fact, sometimes she was the criminal! Phantom thieves, such as Saint Tail, were (and are) also a popular choice in Japan due to the influence of French thief Arsène Lupin.

Thanks to the impact of Naoko Takeuchi's *Pretty Guardian Sailor Moon*, there are more modern *shōjo* manga that play up the superhero-esque, fighting warriors of justice aspects of the magical-girl genre. CLAMP's *Cardcaptor Sakura*, though simpler and less apocalyptic, falls into this category as well, with its quest format and the general sense that its heroine is being tested to ensure that she is strong enough to handle what lies ahead. Reiko Yoshida and Mia Ikumi's *Tokyo Mew Mew* combines magical-girl tropes with environmental issues, as the girls fight to save nature from those who would abuse it.

Despite their superhero themes, most of these series are still very much oriented towards traditional gender roles. *Wedding Peach*'s heroines may fight for truth and justice, but their number one goal is still to become brides. Indeed, *Sailor Moon*'s archetype is rather unusual in that it overtly states that attracting men isn't the primary goal of many of the warriors.

Television anime adaptations of the best magical-girl series have pulled in excellent ratings—so good, in fact, that the industry is now creating more non-*shōjo* magical-girl manga than its counterpart. Don't be fooled by titles such as *Magical Girl Lyrical Nanoha* or *Puella Magi Madoka Magica*. Though these series do attract female fans (as well as children), they are definitely created with a male audience in mind, and their manga series run in magazines for young men. Even a series such as *Pretty Cure*—a Japanese anime franchise that includes multiple spinoffs— is marketed as a children's show while also reaching out to young men. As times change, the boundaries between "girls' manga" and everything else are getting fuzzier, and no genre reflects this quite like the magical-girl genre.

Sports

It must be said, sports manga is a major land-office business in Japan that has entirely failed to catch on in North America. Though there have been a few sports-related *shōnen* series translated into English, none of them have matched the popularity of battle manga like *Naruto* or *Bleach*. And when it comes to *shōjo*, the list is even smaller, including several series that were canceled before they could be completed in English. This is not to diminish *shōjo* sports titles, however, which can be just as inspiring and heartbreaking as their male-oriented counterparts.

The old-school classics of the genre are beloved by anime and manga fans with long memories, even if they've never been officially released over here. Tennis manga *Ace o Nerae!*, better known as *Aim for the Ace!*, is a quintessential 1970s *shōjo* title—one that rivals *Jump* series *The Prince of Tennis* for putting the spotlight on its sport. There are many classic *shōjo* tropes here: the heroine deals with self-confidence issues throughout the entire series, and is constantly on the edge of despair about her lack of ability, her love life, or both. In fact, her love life is one of the main problems, as both her friends and her coach tell her that she has to focus on tennis rather than love—harsh words for a high-school girl!

Another massively influential *shōjo* sports manga is Chikako Urano's *Attack No. 1*, which dates even earlier. Debuting in 1968, it was the first big *shōjo* sports hit, and one of the first big *shōjo* hits, period. Volleyball is the series' sport of choice (and indeed, remains a very popular choice for female sports manga), but the basic premise is similar—a talented but fragile young girl deals with jealous rivals and budding romance, while honing her skills to be the best volleyball player in Japan. Its influence not only spread to other *shōjo* manga (such as the more recent *Crimson Hero*), but even to modern day female volleyball stars, many of whom watched the anime adaptation as children.

As for officially licensed manga in North America dealing with sports, the choices are more limited. The most successful *shōjo* title with sports in it would probably be the romantic comedy *Hana-Kimi*, though it's doubtful that many readers purchased it for the track and field. *Girl Got Game* (released in Japan as *Power!!*, a rare example of an English title being changed to a different English title for North America) is a bit more focused on its heroine's attempts to become a basketball star. Both these titles share a common theme: the girls disguise themselves as boys in order to achieve their dreams.

Less successful were *My Heavenly Hockey Club*, by Ai Morinaga, which struggled with an audience confused by its lack of focus on field hockey (as well as its broad comedy), and *Crimson Hero*, in which the heroine attempts to resurrect a school's girls' volleyball team while dealing with the various men in her life. Both these titles are fairly lengthy (14 and 20 volumes, respectively), and have been put on hiatus by their North American publishers. Shorter *shōjo* sports series fare a bit better, such as the two-volume ice skating manga *Sugar Princess*.

Fantasy

As one of the most popular genres of *shōjo* manga, both here and in Japan, "fantasy" encompasses quite a bit. The genre includes the RPG-inspired swords and giant robots of *Magic Knight Rayearth*, epic romance across alternate worlds in *Fushigi*

Yûgi, and the supernatural action series *Vampire Knight*. Supernatural series are popular in other demographic categories as well, of course, but lend themselves to *shōjo* in particular, with many magazines in Japan devoted either entirely or predominantly to the genre.

Perhaps the most common type of *shōjo* fantasy to make its way to North America is that of the regular high-school girl who suddenly finds herself in another world. This trope lends itself particularly well to long, involved plotting. Besides *Rayearth* and *Fushigi Yûgi*, two great examples of the genre include the seventeen-volume *Haruka: Beyond the Stream of Time* (based on a computer game marketed to women), in which three students are transported to an alternate world similar to Japan's past, and *Red River*, a twenty-eight-volume epic about a young woman who ends up in ancient Mesopotamia, where she must pass as a reincarnation of the goddess Ishtar.

Most of CLAMP's early success was in the fantasy genre; both *RG Veda* and *Tokyo Babylon*, as well as the apocalyptic *X*, feature strange powers, mysterious yet troubled young men, and lots of people dying—but dying gorgeously. These titles, like many mainstream *shōjo* fantasy series, also involve intense relationships between young men—a nod to the popularity of boys' love manga.

Much of the fantasy genre crosses over with romantic drama, and its supernatural creatures are often portrayed as sexy—even unnaturally so. Here, vampires, demons, and angels share troubled pasts, a tendency to lash out at those they love, and the ability to brood beautifully. Kaori Yuki's *Angel Sanctuary* may actually be the pinnacle of the genre, if only for its sense of drama. Featuring incestuous overtones, fallen angels, demonic sexual assaults, and more than one death and resurrection, it narrowly qualifies as acceptable teen content in the West, while its powerful climax handsomely rewards readers who have endured its twenty volumes.

High-School Issues/Realistic

Though most high-school-based *shōjo* focuses on romance, real teenagers deal with more than just first love (and first breakups), and *shōjo* manga addresses these points as well. Issues such as parental abandonment and/or abuse, body issues leading to eating disorders, bullying by other peer groups, and even suicide attempts crop up in *shōjo* manga, providing young girls with similar experiences an opportunity to identify with their protagonists and to feel they aren't alone. Many of these stories are meant for older teens, but not all of them; even younger-skewing *shōjo* magazines deal with bullying, for example.

In North America, several titles dealing with "real-world issues" have been published, although none has been a smashing success. Keiko Suenobu's *Life*, for example, had nine volumes published before the rights were lost. The series, about a high-school girl who begins cutting herself to deal with the pressures of fitting in at a new school, also tackles bullying, attempted suicide, and *enjo kosai* (compensated dating). *Confidential Confessions* was an anthology series that dealt with similar subjects, also bringing up drug abuse and HIV. Popular *shōjo* romance manga (*Gakuen Alice* and *Fruits Basket*, for example) may also address issues like school bullying.

Horror

The desire to be scared has always provided inspiration to popular fiction, and Japan specializes in such frights—particularly those aimed at the *shōjo* audience. *Shōjo* stories tend to be character driven and psychologically motivated—trying to get into the heads of their heroines. In that respect, the horror genre would seem to be tailor made for it. As with many other *shōjo* categories, horror is often merged with other genres, particularly fantasy, mystery, or romance, as in the popular romantic horror series *Vampire Knight*.

One of the purest horror manga to be released in North America is Miyuki Eto's *Hell Girl* (adapted from the anime series of the same name), about desperate young people who sell their souls to Hell in order to get revenge on their tormentors. Setona Mizushiro's *After School Nightmare* is less sadistic, but just as dark, and features some genuinely scary imagery. And Kaori Yuki (*Grand Guignol Orchestra*) has made a career out of gothic horror *shōjo*, complete with incredibly pretty young men and very messy deaths. Luckily, not all horror manga is as bleak and hopeless as these. Yuki Midorikawa's *Natsume's Book of Friends*, for example, deals with a boy who can see monsters and spirits and his attempts to live a normal life and make friends while helping the spirits however he can.

As Japanese girls grow up and become adults, they tend to take their horror titles with them; many *josei* magazines cater to fans of Japanese mysteries and horror with spiritual detectives, ghosts, and terrifying creatures straight out of movies such as *The Ring*.

Triggers

As noted previously, many *shōjo* manga deal with real-life teen issues, and not just the light and fluffy stuff. *Shōjo* manga can involve eating disorders, sexual assault and rape, suicide, classism, and lots and lots of bullying. And it's not just classmates doing the bullying; many popular romance titles involve male love interests who are distant, possessive, and sometimes even verbally or emotionally abusive. Any of these could trigger trauma in a young reader facing similar issues, so it's important to be prepared for this type of content. (And be warned, as in real life, bullies are rarely punished in manga.)

"Shōjo *Manga" That Isn't*

It's been noted that *shōjo* manga can be more than just school romance, including fantasy, sports, horror, and even occasional stories about grownups. Manga genres can be fluid, however, both in Japan and in North America, and often something that appears to be aimed at young girls actually skews much older or may even be targeted for adult males.

A good example of the former is *Butterflies, Flowers,* released in North America on Viz's Shojo Beat imprint. In Japan, this series is a straight-up *josei* office romance—one that ran in the magazine *Petit Comic* (to which readers of *Shōjo Comic* are supposed to graduate once they leave high school). Though the title is shrink wrapped by Viz and rated M for Mature, the imprint alone is a poor guide for parents or librarians curating a teen collection. Similarly, *Honey and Clover,* though innocent enough not to require a mature rating, is also a *josei* title marketed as *shōjo* in North America.

This becomes even more confusing when working with titles that, while they feature cute young girls and no obvious adult content, are marketed to college-age men in Japan. The aesthetic of "*moe*"—being attracted, nonsexually, to cute young girls or teens doing cute young things—influences a significant majority of anime produced today. While its manga equivalent isn't quite as omnipresent, titles such as *Azumanga Daioh* (six female high-school students and their two teachers having eccentric high-school days), *Strawberry Marshmallow* (four twelve-year-olds and one older sister doing the same thing), and *Yotsuba&!* (a man raising a naive yet adorable five-year-old girl) all run in the magazine *Dengeki Daioh*, marketed in Japan to men in their early 20s.

That said, it's the content that's important. If there's nothing objectionable about the title, the intended demographic hardly matters, and *Azumanga* and *Yotsuba&!*, for example, generally can be read even by young girls. (*Strawberry Marshmallow* is another matter.) After all, even *Sailor Moon*, one of the most popular *shōjo* manga in the world, contains scenes that suggest that its 14-year-old heroine and her high-school boyfriend are going further than one might expect. Don't just trust that something that appears to be *shōjo* is automatically appropriate for young readers, regardless of how it is labeled.

~ ~ ~ ~ ~ ~ ~ ~ ~

Section 3: Notable Artists

Osamu Tezuka

Not only called the father of all manga, Tezuka was also dubbed the mother of *shōjo* manga, primarily due to the influence of his classic *Princess Knight*. First appearing in *Shōjo Club* magazine in 1954, the series was reworked and rewritten by Tezuka three times. He also wrote a sequel, *Twin Knight*, featuring the offspring of the original star. In this story, a cherub sent from heaven has mistakenly given the newborn Princess Sapphire a boy's heart, even as she was already born with a girl's heart. Growing up with both the adventurous spirit of a boy and the caring love of a girl, Sapphire struggles with this duality into her teenage years, while the cherub, now exiled from heaven for his mistake, tries desperately to get the male heart back.

Despite what reads as questionable gender politics by modern standards, the series was groundbreaking for Japan in its time. Sapphire dresses as a prince, learns how to fight, and otherwise acts the adventure hero (as long as she's got her boy's heart), which was thrilling for the series' young female readership, and led to innumerable other authors doing the same thing. To this day, cross-dressing and gender play are a common theme in *shōjo* manga, and many classic 1970s *shōjo* romances feature a handsome girl as the school's "prince," skilled in horseback riding, saving waiflike maidens from school bullies, and dying in a conveniently tragic way. Most modern manga fans are familiar with *Revolutionary Girl Utena*, about a sword-fighting girl who wants to be a prince, which deconstructs both the gender politics and the simplistic approach to good and evil found in Tezuka's original work.

Tezuka did write a few other *shōjo* manga in his long and prolific career, though none quite had the same impact as *Princess Knight* (and are not yet available in the West). *Marvelous Melmo* was an early 1970s magica-girl story, in which a 9-year-old girl who has lost her parents is given magical candy that can turn her into a 19-year-old, so that she can better care for her two younger brothers. The series was intended by Tezuka to involve some sex education for young girls (Melmo is still an immature girl inside, but as a 19-year-old must deal with more adult situations), but otherwise was an adventure series for first graders. *Angel's Hill* is an early 1960s fantasy manga that features a mermaid princess, who embarks on a series of increasingly dangerous adventures after being exiled for breaking the rules. Most of Tezuka's *shōjo* manga proved that while he didn't dip into that well often, he was as much of a master as when he wrote for boys and adults.

Year 24 Group

Between 1970 and 1973, a new revolution in manga began, brought about by a loose collection of women all born in approximately the same year—Year 24 of the Showa period, or 1949 in Western terms. Generally speaking, the Year 24 group brought a greater depth of characterization and mood to *shōjo*, showing that the genre could move beyond its childish roots and tackle more meaningful and philosophical themes. In addition, their art style advanced the genre as well. The Year 24 group brought an aesthetic to their manga that was more realistic, more detailed, and more elegant than we'd previously seen. Featuring tall, androgynous heroes and heroines in the latest fashions, the art grew up with the story lines, taking *shōjo* manga into maturity, even as it was still marketed to girls and young women.

Several of these writers' works have been published in North America, although some have been cut short, and most have sold poorly. Yasuko Aoike's *From Eroica with Love* has been running in the magazine *Princess* since 1976. Fifteen of its volumes were released here before its North American publisher folded. Keiko Takemiya's *Kaze to Ki no Uta*, one of the most influential boys' love manga of the late 70s and early 80s, has never been licensed for release in North America. Ironically, the two titles of hers which have been translated in English, *To Terra . . .* and *Andromeda Stories*, are classified as *shōnen*. Similarly, Ryoko Yamagishi's *Shiroi Heya no Futari*, considered one of the urtexts of *yuri* manga, is unavailable to English-speaking readers.

The two artists from this group most well known to Western readers are Riyoko Ikeda and Moto Hagio. Hagio's work has been the most available in North America, published first by Viz (*They Were Eleven* and *A, A'*), and more recently by Fantagraphics, who released the critically acclaimed short story collection *A Drunken Dream and Other Stories* in 2010, and have licensed her boys' love classic *Heart of Thomas* for release in 2013. As for Ikeda, her titles *The Rose of Versailles* and *Oniisama E* (*Brother Dear Brother*) are beloved the world over, though still unpublished in North America. Only the anime adaptation of *Oniisama E* has been made available in English.

As a group, the importance of the Year 24 artists cannot be overstated. They expanded the reach of *shōjo* manga to genres beyond the bounds of high-school romance, and also paved the way for both the boys' love and *yuri* genres.

Naoko Takeuchi

She may have only one really famous work to her name, but what a work! *Bishōjo Senshi Sailor Moon* (*Pretty Guardian Sailor Moon*) transformed the magical-girl genre in Japan in the 1990s, and its anime series, imported to the U.S. and dubbed for young viewers, was even more influential. It would not be an exaggeration to say that a majority of female manga fans in North America were introduced to the medium by way of *Sailor Moon*. The anime series is perhaps better known, but the manga was a bestseller when first released by Tokyopop, and its rerelease in 2011–13 by Kodansha Comics is an even bigger hit, with new volumes consistently topping bestseller charts.

The series transformed the magical-girl genre, which had previously revolved around very youthful fantasies such as becoming an idol singer or princess of a magical kingdom—usually involving changing from a small child into an older teenaged woman. *Sailor Moon*'s heroines, however, were soldiers, ready to use their powers to fight evil, and to sacrifice their lives, if necessary. By taking the basic plot and themes of Japanese *sentai* ("fighting squadron") series—popularized in the West by *Mighty Morphin Power Rangers*—and putting a magical-girl spin on it, Takeuchi allowed her heroines to be more empowered than the genre had ever seen before, and was unapologetic about using them for the greater good.

Sailor Moon's heroine, Usagi Tsukino, was endearing yet fallible—a cute, clumsy girl who got bad grades but nevertheless had a heart big enough to love the entire world. And for those who couldn't identify with her, there were eventually nine other warriors of various personality types. *Sailor Moon*'s fighting squadron managed to battle evil and deal with various real-world problems while still remaining grounded in the teenage lifestyle—celebrities, gossip, and of course boys. However, Takeuchi did not see a need to pair everyone off. By the manga's end, only Usagi has gotten married, the others apparently waiting until they become adults or focusing on other things.

CLAMP

Though known nowadays for manga titles published across all demographic categories, the all-female group of artists known as CLAMP first came to fame for their *shōjo* works. Originally assembled to produce *dōjinshi* in the mid-1980s, by 1993 their number had stabilized at four, and the quartet got down to business producing some of the most memorable manga of the 1990s. Thanks to the strong leadership of writer Nanase Ohkawa and their versatile lead artists, CLAMP do not have a single distinctive art style and their story lines range from such supposed clichés as magical girls (*Cardcaptor Sakura*) and phantom thieves (*Man of Many Faces*) to more serious high fantasy and works with apocalyptic and dark overtones.

It's difficult to choose an archetypal CLAMP manga, as even among just their *shōjo* work, their series cover a wide range of themes. *RG Veda*, a fantasy featuring pretty young men and mythological overtones, was their first big hit. Their trilogy of "CLAMP Campus" works—*Man of Many Faces*, *CLAMP School Detectives*, and

Duklyon: CLAMP School Defenders—was a break from the serious tone of that series, and was predominantly light and silly in nature.

But while those were popular, their next major title, X (along with its seven-volume prequel, Tokyo Babylon), was a breakout smash—one that they are still best known for today. It has spawned an anime as well as a movie, and builds inexorably towards a tragic, inevitable apocalyptic showdown. Unfortunately, due in part to its artwork portraying rubble and destruction in a nation known for earthquakes, and in part to conflicts with its publisher, Kadokawa, the series has been on hiatus since 2003 and may never see a proper conclusion.

For Kodansha, CLAMP created two more enduring series. *Magic Knight Rayearth* combined the *shōjo* fantasy of "schoolgirls in another world" with common role-playing elements, as well as magical armor that looked suspiciously like giant robots. The month after *Rayearth* ended, in 1996, CLAMP began *Cardcaptor Sakura*, which has become perhaps the most well-known magical-girl manga after *Pretty Guardian Sailor Moon*. Like the *CLAMP School* series, *Cardcaptor Sakura* displayed the group's lighthearted side. Sakura, Syaoran, and Tomoyo are some of their most lovable characters, and the series has been reprinted in North America three different times.

CLAMP have always pushed the boundaries of genre; after two short but solid series for Kadokawa in the late 90s (*Wish*, about angels, demons, and reincarnation; and *Suki: A Like Story*, whose relationship between an almost comically naive girl and her older bodyguard would later influence their *seinen* series *Chobits*), they decided to branch out to other demographics. In fact, their last series for a *shōjo* magazine, *Legal Drug*, recently restarted and moved to a magazine for adult men—with no actual change in content or mood—thus proving two things: that genre is fluid in Japan, and that CLAMP are influential hit makers no matter what they write.

Natsuki Takaya

Like Naoko Takeuchi and *Sailor Moon*, Natsuki Takaya is best known in North America (and indeed in Japan) for only one series. But again, when it's one of the biggest manga sellers in the entire world, attention must be paid. Beginning as a cute romantic comedy about a teenaged girl and her wealthy neighbors—a cursed family who turn into animals when hugged by someone of the opposite sex—*Fruits Basket* grows into an epic, serious drama, traversing some very dark paths in the human psyche. Even its lead, maligned by readers early on as the sort of saccharine *shōjo* heroine who heals everyone she touches through the power of niceness, is revealed to be masking her true fears and feelings, and breaking down her emotional barriers becomes the key to saving all the others. Over the course of the series, *Fruits Basket* features not only traditional *shōjo* material like love triangles and cute animals, but also tackles issues of psychological and emotional abuse, from school bullying to outright torture.

Of course, things do work out in the end—indeed, some of the series' most seemingly evil characters get the happiest endings. Though the manga deals with meaningful abuse issues, it does offer hope for the future and typical *shōjo* happy endings. (Unlike *Sailor Moon*, *Fruits Basket* does endeavor to pair up nearly every character with a lifelong romantic partner.)

Fruits Basket is Takaya's longest series to date in Hakusensha's *Hana to Yume* magazine, where she has been published since her debut in 1992. Two other short series, *Phantom Dream* and *Tsubasa: Those with Wings*, were also published in North America by Tokyopop, but neither displayed the same addictive soap-opera quality as *Fruits Basket*. The eleven-volume series *Hoshi Wa Utau*, published after *Fruits Basket* in Japan, is a quieter, more melancholy work. Takaya's newest fantasy series, *Liselotte to Majo no Mori*, features a forest full of witches and is currently ongoing. Neither is yet available in English.

Arina Tanemura

In general, fans of manga in North America tend to follow genres or titles rather than authors. Sure, *Fruits Basket* may have been a megahit, but when Tokyopop released Takaya's earlier works, the sales were not nearly as strong. And no one's chasing down any of Naoko Takeuchi's other titles, either. So when virtually every work of a single author has been licensed for North American release, she obviously deserves attention. Arina Tanemura is such an author. Though sales of her work may never match those of *Fruits Basket* or other top-selling *shōjo* manga, she has her own likable brand going for her—a series of somewhat fantastical dramatic romances, usually with tinges of a magical-girl-style plot line.

With the exception of her most recent (and yet-unlicensed) title, Tanemura writes for one magazine: *Ribon*, Shueisha's flagship publication for young girls. Unlike many other *shōjo* magazines in Japan that really cater to older teenagers, *Ribon* genuinely is for younger readers from 8 to 12 years old. Tanemura's artwork suits the "cute" sensibility of the magazine, accompanied by medium-length romances with catchy plots. Her heroes and heroines are likable, spunky, and easy to root for.

Tanemura's biggest hits (they both earned anime adaptations) are her phantom thief story *Kamikaze Kaito Jeanne* (released by the now-defunct CMX) from 1999 and her supernatural romance *Full Moon o Sagashite* from 2002 (released on Viz's Shojo Beat imprint). Both proved popular enough for Viz to grab up her other works, including the psychic-magical-girl manga *I.O.N.*, futuristic time-powered fantasy *Time Stranger Kyoko*, and romantic soap opera *Gentlemen's Alliance Cross*, which makes up for a lack of fantasy by offering up Tanemura's most intriguing love triangle to date.

None of Tanemura's works are masterpieces, and they don't command the same level of fandom as the best *shōjo* series on the market. But she's a sure seller, and you always know you'll get a pretty good yarn when you pick up one of her works. Most of all, in a market increasingly occupied by mature *shōjo* titles aimed at a higher age bracket, most of Tanemura's works can be read by the same audience as in Japan—girls ages 8 to 12 who want to read the adventures of a spunky young heroine with her choice of cute young guys.

CHAPTER 4

Seinen Manga
by Ed Chavez

Section 1: What Is *Seinen*?

Men's manga, known in Japan as *seinen* manga, is currently the largest category of comics published in Japan. While it was not formally marketed under that label until the late 1960s, this sector of the manga market has been critical to the industry since Japan began publishing its own comics in the late half of the 19th century. The term "*seinen*" was first coined in reference to comics in the 1960s, as a reaction to the declining and increasingly difficult-to-access *gekiga* market. Before "*seinen*" was used, most comics for adults were either *gekiga* or editorial comics called *Jiji Manga*.

Seinen is distinguished amongst the world of Japanese comics as encompassing the broadest themes for the most diverse readership, while employing a wide net of talent from across the country and the world—crossing barriers of gender and age. *Seinen* utilizes a number of art styles. The stories told could cover practically any topic conceived for film, television, or prose. Works can be comical or lyrical. They may be short works of nonfiction or vast fantastic narratives set in any time in history or the far future. *Seinen*'s restrictions are limited to the demands of its readers. And yet at the same time, because around a quarter of Japan's publishing industry is based on comics, the hyperfocus on niche genres seen in certain anthologies, such as golf comics and mahjong comics, may not be possible in any other comics market globally.

Seinen at its core is accessible, contemporary, and entertaining. It must be affordable and readily available. When *seinen* titles become too difficult to find in stores, they and their artists are often forced into the realm of alternative comics. If works are too esoteric or extreme in their violence or sex, they may be pushed into the adult comics industry, the Young Comics sector (a subset of *seinen* that caters to hot-blooded older teens, often characterized by violent or erotic content) or *dōjinshi* (self-publishing).

Because of these principles, it may surprise the uninitiated to see comics that appear to be for elementary-school readers sold alongside works clearly for readers in their middle age. Such a wide range of demographics and material is typical when *seinen* anthologies and imprints are not genre specific. This accessibility has long led to *seinen* achieving critical acclaim worldwide. It also has become a great source for media inspiration, as many of these works have been adapted for television and film across the globe.

For many of the same reasons, *seinen* has also found itself amidst quite a bit of controversy both in and outside of Japan. Because social norms vary from country to country, some subject matter in *seinen* comics has caused controversy. Imagery has been a topic of even greater concern. The *seinen* readership tends to be more mature, with most readers in their adulthood. Nudity and violence vary from publisher to publisher and publication to publication. Self-enforced standards are just being codified in Japan, but even then these "restrictions" are generally only taking Japan's domestic market into consideration.

However, even with a few hurdles to overcome, the market for *seinen* content in North America appears to be seeing a renaissance. Almost every American publisher is now releasing this material—to more and more readers—in hopes of further expanding manga literacy as seen previously in Asia and parts of Europe.

Most scholarly writing on manga will direct manga's origins back to *ukiyo-e* (woodblock prints). When looking at the works of the 1800s in particular, many of which not only continued to render images of the people of Japan—from sumo wrestlers to *kabuki* actors and the beautiful women of the time—but also images of the Japanese revolution and laborers in the fields and merchant quarters, it is not difficult to see the influence on modern men's comics.

However, it would take nearly a century for *seinen*-style content to be found readily again.

~~~~~~~~~

Section 2: History of *Seinen*

Gekiga

Manga's fortunes have long been tied not so much to design or even genre, but to distribution. While distribution for comics was improving quickly, Japan's size and geographical circumstances (mountainous with many small islands) made providing weekly content nationwide difficult. Small local publishers and printers provided alternatives by working with local businesses to develop a rental comic industry. At these shops, customers could purchase anthologies or newspapers. They also had the option of renting reprints of existing comic books from major cities like Tokyo or Osaka, or original comics from local authors and independent publishing houses.

As rental comic shops began to establish themselves in their communities, the stores would soon find out what their specific clientele were demanding. Like most bookstores, they would take on a specific flavor or feel for specific genres and work closely with independent publishers to sell, or even at times commission, anthologies or individual works to cater to their unique readers' tastes.

Gekiga would develop out of this industry, as many of the rental comics readers were looking for comics similar in tone to the films they were watching (or simply hearing about). *Gekiga* comics featured samurai and ninja tales, like many kids' comics, along with cowboy-and-Indian westerns, science fiction–infused horror, noir-style mysteries, and erotic dramas. *Gekiga* initially had visuals that looked very comical and childish like its predecessors, but those designs evolved rather quickly over time. Eventually, many artists developed a heavier sense of realism. Some of the finest draftsmen of the last century came out of this movement.

By the late 1960s, *gekiga* had grown increasingly difficult both to sell and consume. Its works had become more visually experimental, shedding the minimalist designs used historically for children's comics, and straying too far from the norms of comics publishing to be accepted by the masses, let alone the publishing establishment. Furthermore, their stories were becoming increasingly violent and sexually charged—

heavily influenced by the boom in film noir and explorative genre films of the times. The *gekiga* market also suffered from lack of distribution systems in the aftermath of World War II. Its books were generally available only regionally with limited print runs through rental libraries, which could disappear as quickly as the books they made available. In contrast, *seinen* works, like children's comics, found national distribution, as they were mainly produced by established publishing houses.

Gekiga continues to be published today. Many of the current designs tend still to look much like what was being produced in the 1960s and 70s, and the stories tend to be very similar as well. However, the concept of *gekiga* has changed. *Gekiga* now is almost synonymous with exploitative fiction, covering many of the same subgenres. To some, it is considered softcore pornography, as many of the works regularly feature nudity. *Gekiga*'s distribution has been greatly limited in Japan, and most of its readers tend to be older adults and people in the suburbs or more rural locales. For this reason, these books and anthologies are generally found in convenience stores, shelved next to alcohol and pornography.

The Seinen *Boom*

The term "*seinen*" (adolescent or young adult) was first used by a small magazine publisher named Futabasha. Futabasha had previously worked in the field of scandal journalism, and their first foray into the world of comics was the men's comic *Manga Action* in July 1967. By distinguishing itself as a *seinen* publication, *Action* was a pioneer in the field, as it was clearly setting itself apart from the *shōnen* and *shōjo* comics that had dominated manga publishing since the 1940s. Futabasha attracted up-and-coming talent from both the *shōnen* and *shōjo* industries and the *gekiga* movement to write for a mainstream young-adult audience that was desperately looking for more sophisticated entertainment.

Unlike *gekiga* before it, *seinen* was quickly adopted by practically every comics publisher in the country within the next 15 years. After Japan's rapid postwar reconstruction, publishers and distributors were now developed enough to ship out anthology magazines—often featuring dozens of unique series—nationwide, every week or every other week. This provided affordable and accessible entertainment to a nation where TV viewing was not prolific until the mid-1970s and movie ticket prices had long been between $15 and $20 a ticket.

By 1980, even with an established television culture, there were nearly four dozen *seinen* anthologies in publication, and that total would reach nearly ninety by the turn of the twenty-first century. It was in the late 1970s and early 1980s when men's comics overtook boys' and girls' comics in publications and anthologies. While the most popular works were still generally for children (due to long-established marketing mechanisms including cartoons, toys, games, and merchandise), *seinen* comics were still being consumed and produced at an increasingly fast rate.

Much like the end of the *gekiga* era, when Japan entered its *seinen* boom, many of the industry's biggest names made the transition to write for this new demographic. Rumiko Takahashi, creator of *Ranma ½* and *Urusei Yatsura*, would pen her romance *Maison Ikkoku* to help launch Shogakukan's new *seinen* anthology *Big Comic Spirits*. *Shōnen* fantasy author Yu Koyama crossed over full time to pen the seminal ninja tale *Asumi*. Shigeru Mizuki, one of the fathers of modern manga (and a former rental comic artist), had long drawn children's folktales of goblins and spirits (such as in his work *Kitaro*), but by the 1990s, he was shifting his perspective towards a much older readership by drawing personal stories about his time in World War II and his experiences with Japan's occult mythology.

It was at this point that *seinen* manga greatly expanded its position in the marketplace. One step taken early on was to begin producing works to complement the tastes of Japan's developed middle class. In the 1980s, Japan was deep in its economic bubble, so stories of office workers were commonplace. The hobbies of middle-class men and women inspired dozens of hit properties. A taste for gourmet cuisine led to *Oishinbo*. More humble meals inspired *Cooking Papa*. (Both titles have been running regularly since the early 1980s.)

Possibly the most iconic *seinen* character has been Kosaku Shima, star of the *Section Chief Kosaku Shima* comic series. In that series, a humble office worker climbs the business ladder (eventually becoming CEO) over a nearly 30-year career depicted in weekly comics serialization. Golf, fishing, gambling, baseball, and even American politics have been common themes since the beginning. These genres complement the more fantasy-based genres found in mainstream manga.

From *seinen*'s early days, works such as Monkey Punch's *Lupin III* (inspired by the Arsène Lupin stories) introduced a more nuanced and sophisticated form of visual media to the world. Long before Spiegelman penned *Maus*, and as Eisner was coining the term "graphic novel," *seinen* artists were writing works with mature themes in long form. Tales of espionage, child rearing, office work, or even sports were being introduced alongside more traditional *shōnen* and *gekiga* themes like mysteries, future-looking science fiction, and samurai period pieces, allowing producers to explore a range of genres for their networks or movie studios.

The increased use of long-form narratives would compel budding film directors to take on these projects to transform Japan's animation industry, as comics' serialization provided ideal source material for television's episodic programming. At the same time, with many *seinen* artists also dabbling in animation, Japan saw a brief explosion of direct-to-video animation shorts directed or designed by comic artists.

Due to that abundance of content, *seinen* manga has produced the largest volume of content within the comics industry since the 1990s. In the 1980s and 90s, trends like science fiction and action provided plenty of new source material for animated film and serialized cartoons. By the 2000s, *seinen* was revitalizing Japan's live-action drama industry by providing ideas for prime-time programming, from hard-boiled dramas to situation comedies. This trend eventually spread to the rest of East Asia. As international licensing becomes more common, properties like Tadashi Agi's *Drops of God* and Garon Tsuchiya's *Old Boy* are being acquired in Asia and North America, respectively, for localization in those markets.

The final step for *seinen* was global expansion. *Shōnen* and *shōjo* properties were already becoming accepted in Europe, South America, and across Asia. Some of those properties were beginning to trickle into the U.S. However, *seinen* was just starting to establish itself, and its mature themes might have posed problems if positioned for Saturday-morning cartoon blocks or traditional animation-based cable networks like Disney or Nickelodeon. But the world was not to be denied the animation boom of the 1980s, and while *shōnen* properties such as *Captain Tsubasa* and *Saint Seiya* were driving forces globally, *seinen* properties took command in North America.

Directors such as Mamoru Oshii, Katsuhiro Otomo, and Satoshi Kon would all come to adapt *seinen* works in the 1980s and 90s. Each had experience within the comics industry. Like Osamu Tezuka before them, these directors took on subject matter that inspired them as youths. Tezuka, inspired by Kitazawa and Takarazuka theater, created comical works for everyone to enjoy. Now, this new generation was looking to the films of the 1970s and early 80s to reimagine science fiction and psycho thrillers in ways rarely seen before, in Japan or abroad. This proved to be the catalyst for manga and *seinen*, catapulting these comics from works that were occasionally translated by small circles into a viable leg of the North American comics industry.

Seinen *in the United States*

In the United States, *seinen* holds a very unique place regarding manga culture. While the first manga available in the U.S. was a *shōnen* title (Kenji Nakazawa's *Barefoot Gen*), the vast majority of titles initially published in English were *seinen* properties. As many of these comics had themes and tones similar to those in the science-fiction scene at the time, it was not uncommon to see American comics publishers attempting to introduce Japanese works to their existing readership. *Seinen* manga's connection to the blossoming Japanese animation industry further cemented this foothold in the West. Many initial properties such as *Akira* and *Dominion* found cult followings in the West.

For more than a decade, manga in the U.S. was almost entirely *seinen*. And they were published in a format very much influenced by American sensibilities. Unlike their counterparts in the Far East, U.S. publishers released manga in monthly magazine format. Each issue contained one or more chapters of a given series. Some American publishers colorized the comics to appeal to the tastes of their readership. *Akira* and Rumiko Takahashi's *Urusei Yatsura* were two properties that received this rare treatment. Almost all manga at the time were reproduced in a mirrored ("flopped") format to conform to Western reading conventions, as opposed to the right-to-left standard used in Japan.

Most publishers who localized manga initially were small imprints or independent studios. In the case of *Golgo 13*, it was a Japanese company, LEED, Ltd., that attempted to break into the American market. Because of this, many licensed manga were short lived or extremely difficult to find.

Dark Horse Comics changed all of that. When Mike Richardson founded Dark Horse in 1986, he did so with artists in mind. Artists retained their rights and dictated the direction of their properties. This model was similar to the Japanese market, in which creators generally hold all copyrights to their works, so it was not much of a stretch for this new publisher from Oregon to work with some of manga's biggest names and brands. Often working in cooperation with the late Toren Smith's Studio Proteus, Dark Horse has released a number of *seinen* works, including Kosuke Fujishima's *Oh My Goddess!*, the longest-running manga in the United States. Properties such as Kentaro Miura's *Berserk* and Kohta Hirano's *Hellsing* have sold tens of thousands of units in the U.S., making them some of the best-known comic brands in the last ten years.

After Dark Horse's foray into manga, many other publishers followed suit. Around the same time Dark Horse entered the manga business, another company from San Francisco called Viz Entertainment (now known as Viz Media) would also make its move. The company, founded in 1986 through investment by Japanese publisher Shogakukan Inc., initially released (in cooperation with former U.S. indie publisher Eclipse Comics) *seinen* works such as Sanpei Shirato's *The Legend of Kamui* and Koike's *Mai, the Psychic Girl*.

In 1997, Viz premiered their first *seinen* anthology, *PULP*. The monthly magazine introduced readers to a different brand of manga and Japanese culture by way of essays, articles, and an eclectic collection of comics that very much mirrored the breadth of Japan's *seinen* market. Ultimately, the project proved to be ahead of its time, and the manga boom of the early 2000s would be driven by *shōjo* comics. Nevertheless, Viz would continue to publish these works, even devoting two new imprints to this content in succeeding years.

The first of these imprints was Viz Signature. Signature replaced the PULP line after the anthology was dissolved, and it quickly became one of the most critically acclaimed imprints in English-translated manga. Most Signature properties have been *seinen* comics, though a few have been alternative comics. In 2009, Signature spun off its own subdivision called IKKI, releasing properties exclusively from Shogakukan's *IKKI* anthology.

As noted previously, *seinen* manga has come full circle, particularly in the West, bringing over content from the early days of the demographic, as well as the latest titles. This phenomenon is somewhat unique to this sector of the manga industry, as very little has been translated from the deeper archives of *shōnen* and *shōjo*. Even less can be found of early *josei* (women's) comics, despite having a history almost as long as *seinen*.

For nearly a decade, publishers outside of the manga-publishing realm have been taking on such works as well, and their success with many of these properties has changed the landscape for manga even further.

One of the first publishers to make this step was Last Gasp. This San Francisco–based publisher and distributor has become known for releasing nonconventional comics, and their manga have the same tone. With titles ranging from violent horror-comedies like *Tokyo Zombie* (Yusaku Hanakuma) and *Pure Trance* (Junko Mizuno) to the sentimental look at the aftermath of the Hiroshima bombing *Town of Evening Calm, Country of Cherry Blossoms* (Fumiyo Kono), Last Gasp has been effective in introducing manga to readers and vendors who may not have made such thematic associations with the medium before.

Montreal's Drawn & Quarterly put *gekiga* in the spotlight again, garnering reviews of Yoshihiro Tatsumi's very adult, sexually graphic work from some of the biggest names in American media. To see NPR and PEN both discussing manga titles from the 1960s and 70s was not imaginable ten years ago.

Japanese novel publisher Vertical established their manga line by releasing Osamu Tezuka's *seinen* works in a prestige format (later used by Drawn & Quarterly and PictureBox), and have since collected three Eisners in less than ten years. Vertical's line now releases upwards of eight manga properties a year, two-thirds of which hail from *seinen*'s broad spectrum. Titles like *Chi's Sweet Home* (Konami Kanata), a comic about cat adoption, are sold alongside their Japanese courtesan drama *Sakuran*.

~ ~ ~ ~ ~ ~ ~ ~ ~

Section 3: Mature Content

Manga in America now has developed a nearly thirty-year history, and *seinen* has played a major role all along the way. Now every manga publisher in North America publishes *seinen* regularly. Men's comics are being written about in publications such as *Time Magazine* and the *New York Times*. And adaptations of these works are regularly appearing on The Sy-Fy Network and The Cartoon Network. However, these comics are also at risk of misinterpretation.

Seinen's topics are mature and their readership is intended to be sophisticated. These properties in general are labeled and rated. They are priced higher than manga for teens. And more often than not, more adult-leaning manga are even shrink wrapped to prevent underage readers from accessing such books easily. This self-imposed policing is done almost exclusively for manga in North America. And yet there is still potential for misinterpretation. *Seinen* is manga's highest form of narrative expression and, like film and television, it can challenge audiences with its imagery.

~ ~ ~ ~ ~ ~ ~ ~ ~

Section 4: Notable Artists

Osamu Tezuka

Osamu Tezuka has often been credited as the godfather of manga. Having penned thousands of pages and hundreds of books throughout his career, he is said to have developed many manga genres and to have created many of the techniques that distinguish manga from comics from other cultures.

His position in *seinen* is generally underappreciated in the West, despite the fact that most of his translated works fall into this broad category. Tezuka's major works were created for younger readers. *Astro Boy*, *Black Jack*, and *Princess Knight* hold such a high position amongst the Japanese that most of his adult works have been neglected. Throughout his later career, Tezuka's *seinen* catalog vaulted his name from mythical figure to one of the most recognized artists in comics worldwide. He is a three-time Eisner Award winner, and practically every one of his *seinen* works has received recognition outside of Japan, beginning with Viz's edition of *Adolf* (a.k.a. *Message to Adolf*) in 1995 and *Phoenix* in 2002, and in recent years through publishers such as Vertical and Tonkam (Europe).

Covering a range of topics, Tezuka's *seinen* catalog remains as topical now as it was in the 1970s. Over the years, American publishers have released his biography of the Buddha, his take on expansion of communism in Asia, a romance told through Greek mythology, and a terrorism-themed thriller—each receiving award nominations and critical acclaim. The success of Tezuka's works, often presented in prestige hardcover format, has opened the doors for other classic works not only to be published in the U.S. by nontraditional manga publishers, but to be recognized as works of literature by the public at large.

Yasuji Kitazawa

Yasuji Kitazawa, known affectionately as Rakuten by most, was heavily influenced by comics from an early age. In his twenties, he was exposed to the works of an Australian illustrator named Frank Arthur Nankivell. Nankivell, a trained artist, traveled Japan and briefly made a living for himself selling cartoons in a country where woodblock prints still had some cultural relevance. Nankivell would eventually move to America to complete his studies before joining *Puck* magazine in the early part of the 20th century, but before he left, Nankivell made his mark on a young Kitazawa.

Discovered by publisher (and influential modernizer) Yukichi Fukuzawa in 1895, the then-nineteen-year-old was hired by a new publishing company, Box of Curiosity. This weekly English-language newspaper firm from Yokohama would introduce a world of European and American comics to Japan's young talent, with guidance from Nankivell.

Kitazawa moved on to the Jiji Press in 1899. This exposure to the world of journalism took his works into a more focused direction, and from that point he pursued comics from a more editorial perspective. In 1902, Kitazawa launched his own cartoon take on the news, *Jiji Manga* (Comics of the times). Kitazawa shared the news of the world through comics format, much like what was being seen in Britain and America, and his new position in the world of publishing exposed him to other comics of the time including *The Katzenjammer Kids, Buster Brown,* and *Happy Hooligan.*

A few years later, Kitazawa further expanded his comics crusade when he launched his own comics anthology, *Tokyo Puck*. Inspired by the original *Puck* from St. Louis (for which his friend Nankivell would later draw), the Tokyo edition was truly international. Kitazawa's *Puck*, filled with satirical, politically infused comics, was sold across East Asia and translated into English and Chinese. He continued publication for ten years, before returning to the news with Jiji Press and *Jiji Manga*. Along the way, the era for manga finally arrived, thanks to the efforts of a man who realized that comics were much more than just entertainment.

Takao Saito

While North American readers have been swayed into crediting Yoshihiro Tatsumi as the father of *gekiga*, many in Japan might make an argument for Takao Saito. There may be others, too, who could stake claim to that title, but Saito has held on to the *gekiga* flag for much longer than any, and has continued to be at the vanguard of a movement almost exclusive to the 1960s.

Saito, like many artists in the *gekiga* movement, grew up in the Osaka region of Japan. Living in the region where Osamu Tezuka lived was a godsend to many aspiring comic artists. And Saito, like Tatsumi, took advantage of this opportunity to occasionally take tutelage from the master (who was not much older than this new wave). But it was quickly evident to Saito, and several of his colleagues, that they could not directly compete with the likes of Tezuka in the market.

The rental market industry put *gekiga* artists in a unique position. However, even that subsect was becoming too broad and too competitive. Saito decided to go in his own direction. He developed the Gekiga Atelier with Yoshihiro Tatsumi and six other artists in 1958. Together they would create, edit, and publish works in their own *gekiga* aesthetic. According to Saito, "they conceptualized a world that was completely different from Tezuka's."

By 1960, Saito and a few of his Atelier partners would separate to launch Saito Productions. From this point on, Saito took on a new position as a conceptual artist and author, while still directing the artistic vision of the group. His company would eventually employ up to seventeen people, each drawing and writing in the *gekiga* style. However, the group's ambitions were beyond *gekiga*'s limitations. Instead, they initially worked in the realm of *shōnen*—toning down their stories while still maintaining more realistic designs and general themes. Saito's stories were filled with Asian fantasies, espionage tales, and dramatizations of historical figures.

His most recognized work is *Golgo 13*. This tale of a cosmopolitan hit man was one of the first *seinen* manga, and is the longest-running men's title in manga history (debuting in 1969 and still running today). *Golgo* is a topical take on revisionist history, in which Saito retells current events through the eyes of an assassin, Duke Togo. *Golgo* was also one of the first manga to be translated into English. It was originally translated and copublished by Saito's own publishing company, LEED, Ltd. LEED continues to publish *gekiga* works today, though now exclusively in Japanese. In North America, Viz Media released selected stories from *Golgo 13*, reigniting a small boom in reprints of manga previously translated in the 1980s and 90s.

Kazuo Koike

Possibly no one has written more controversial and titillating works than Kazuo Koike. If Takao Saito represents the image of *gekiga*, then Kazuo Koike has been its voice. Koike has been writing some of manga's most mature works since the 1970s, working with many of the industry's best artists along the way. His breakthrough work, *Lone Wolf and Cub*, not only continues to be an iconic work in Japan, but was considered to be one of the flag bearers for manga worldwide for nearly a decade, earning awards and recognition across the globe decades after its premiere.

Koike joined Saito Productions in the late 1960s. There, he worked briefly on *Golgo* as a writer, before breaking off to launch his own venture in 1970. Two years later, with his own collaborative, Koike Shoin Corp., he would begin writing a number of inspired works with some of *gekiga*'s most respected artists.

Lone Wolf and Cub, drawn by Eisner Award winner Goseki Kojima, was his breakthrough work. It was a historical fantasy in the tone of B-list samurai films. However, this tale of revenge was far more epic in structure, eventually incorporating historical figures and inspiring a series of live-action films. *Lone Wolf's* success would lead to revisionist history titles such as *Path of the Assassin*, a comic retelling of the legendary ninja Hattori Hanzo, and sexy, vengeance-laden *Lady Snowblood*, the inspiration for American director Quentin Tarantino's *Kill Bill* movies.

Koike's works were filled with sexuality, violence, and a sense of narrative anarchy. His story *The Color of Rage* reimagines both slavery in America and the Japanese revolution. One of his most popular works, *Crying Freeman*, tackles Chinese triads and poses them against Japan's growing bubble economy. Koike would even write a version of Marvel's *Hulk* set in Japan.

Koike is still writing comics—primarily *seinen* or *gekiga* works—but most of his time now is spent as an educator. In the 1970s, he launched a comics course for mentoring young talent in the concepts of comics creation. Among his disciples are many of manga's biggest names of the 1980s and 90s, including Rumiko Takahashi, Keisuke Itagaki, and Hideyuki Kikuchi. Koike has also received three Eisner Awards for his works, placing him in rare company amongst comic writers published in the United States.

Katsuhiro Otomo

The poster boy for *seinen*, globally, is probably Katsuhiro Otomo. While other artists have challenged his position in later years, very few comics creators in history have been as decorated and have sold as many books as Otomo has since his debut in the mid-1970s.

Inspired by Hollywood New Wave film and comics—particularly works by Moebius and Shotaro Ishinomori—Otomo began submitting manuscripts to comics publishers in his teens. By the time he was twenty, Otomo was drawing short stories for small publishers. His breakthrough work, in 1980, was *Domu: A Child's Dream*, drawn for Futabasha's *Manga Action*. This tale of a psychic duel in a housing project fascinated Japanese readers, and earned Otomo a Seiun Award (Japan's equivalent of the Science Fiction and Fantasy Writers of America's Nebula Awards) in 1983.

Otomo's works tend to be filled with action and dystopian settings. Young characters are often rebelling against authoritarian systems—themes that resonate with readers across the globe. Whether making the connection to youth movements in Eastern-bloc Europe or to technological and economic advances in Japan and the United States, Otomo's works struck a chord with a new generation of readers at a time when comics and animation were growing in acceptance in many countries.

Otomo was far more than just a comic artist. He was also a character designer working in Japan's animation industry. With the success of his next major work, *Akira*, a committee of producers in Japan collaborated to fund Otomo's biggest project yet. The film *Akira* would have one of the largest budgets ever for a film in Japan—$11 million—and would receive international recognition. Otomo directed the adaptation of his cyberpunk story set in a futuristic Tokyo to rave reviews, cementing his position amongst a global subculture. Roger Ebert considers it one of the best animated films of all time, and metacritics continue to rank this film high within that category today.

Otomo now focuses on animation instead of comics, but his impact is still felt worldwide. He has won two Eisner Awards and two Harvey Awards, and was awarded the French *Ordre des Arts et des Lettres* in 2005. In 2012, Otomo was entered into the Eisner Hall of Fame for his contributions to the comic arts.

Shirow Masamune

Shirow Masamune's position in the history of manga cannot be denied. When considering the growth of manga (and *seinen* specifically) in the United States, he stands among rarified company as a bestseller and trendsetter. Almost all of his works have been translated into English, and they have all achieved success in a variety of formats and reprints since the early 1990s. However, his fame may not be entirely attributed to his translated comics (most of them translated by Dark Horse Comics), but rather to the adaptation of one of his more experimental works, *Ghost in the Shell*.

Shirow made his name with tech-heavy science fiction. Many of his concepts and designs were straight out of *Blade Runner* and other influential cyberpunk works from the 1980s and 90s. And while his works *Dominion* and *Appleseed* were received with decent fanfare, *Ghost in the Shell* was a completely different animal. All three works were adapted for TV and film; all three saw limited distribution in the United States and abroad. However, while *Dominion* was a staple on cable television and *Appleseed* made its way to VHS retail, *Ghost in the Shell* saw its run in art-house movie theaters.

The *Ghost in the Shell* film was a sensation by the standards of Japanese animation in North America at the time, where even limited distribution was a rarity. And the property is well received to this day, earning high ratings on numerous metacritic websites.

While Shirow did create the source material for the film, he was not actively involved in its production. That credit mainly goes to the director, Mamoru Oshii. However, there is no denying that Shirow, unlike the majority of artists to come after him, immediately resonated with a global audience on all levels, with his rich, futuristic designs and his comical (yet action-filled) cyberpunk narratives.

Naoki Urasawa

Naoki Urasawa made his comics debut in 1983 upon graduating from college with a degree in economics. Like many comic artists his age, he was raised on the manga of Osamu Tezuka. He would read Tezuka's stories as a child and then draw his own versions of Astro Boy and Jungle Emperor Leo. In college, however, his tastes changed and he began to take inspiration from film noir and the manga new wave that Katsuhiro Otomo was developing.

By the time Urasawa made his debut, he had a distinct style built upon some of the finer points of his predecessors. His characters were timeless and memorable. He had developed his own star system (a process initiated by Tezuka, in which artists would develop a cast of cartoon actors they would then recast across different comics). And unlike Otomo or Saito before him, Urasawa was willing to embrace *seinen* as a whole, using his ability to draw noir-styled murder mysteries and tennis-themed romance comedies with the same measured hand, considering narrative before sensationalism. These techniques allowed him to develop long-form properties that surprise rather than offend, while still being impactful—much like Tezuka's work in the 1960s and 70s.

Urasawa's accessibility has also translated to critical acclaim outside of Japan. Five of his nine works have been translated in North America, where he won an Eisner Award in 2011. Seven of those works have been translated into French, and Urasawa received the first *Prix de la série* at the Angoulême International Comics Festival.

CHAPTER 5

Josei Manga
by Shaenon Garrity

Section 1: What Is *Josei*?

Of the four major publishing categories of manga, *josei*, or comics for women, is the smallest and the least represented in the American market. As of this writing, only a relative handful of *josei* titles has been published in English, especially compared to the flood of *shōjo* manga in recent decades. However, as the American manga readership ages, the demand for manga aimed at adult women is likely to grow.

In Japan, the first major manga for women appeared in the 1970s, at the same time that *shōjo* manga was coming into its own and *shōjo* readers were starting to grow up and demand more mature reading material. By the 1980s, *josei* manga had found an audience, especially catching on with young female office workers who, like their male counterparts, needed reading material for the daily subway commute. By the 1990s, there were over 50 magazines dedicated to *josei* manga, with a total circulation of over 120 million.

Romance oriented but more sexually frank than *shōjo* manga, the *josei* manga serialized in magazines like *YOU* and *Be Love* soon developed a reputation for cheap, sleazy romance fiction aimed at office ladies and bored housewives, the manga equivalent of Harlequin romance novels. (In fact, Harlequin's Japanese imprint, Ohzora Shuppan, eventually launched its own line of *josei* manga in the 1990s.)

In the late 1980s, the more explicit *josei* manga split off into their own category of openly pornographic manga for women, often called "ladies' comics" or *redicomi*. *Redicomi* were popular enough to earn a skewering in the 1980s satirical manga

Even a Monkey Can Draw Manga, which sardonically compares the stereotypical bored-married-woman-searching-for-sexual-fulfillment plot to a game of Tetris. The heyday of *redicomi* has passed, most *redicomi* magazines having gone out of business in the manga recession of the mid-1990s, but *Comic Amour*, the most popular *redicomi* magazine, is still going strong, with an estimated readership of almost half a million women.

Meanwhile, mainstream *josei* grew more sophisticated and varied, aiming at a younger, hipper audience of college girls and young career women. Like Western "chick lit," modern *josei* runs the gamut from frothy romance to frank erotica to realistic (and often comedic) stories of modern women juggling careers, relationships, and family life. Popular *josei* magazines include *Be Love*, which features mostly traditional romance-and-relationship stories, and *Flowers*, which often includes historical dramas, adventure stories, and science fiction alongside more down-to-earth fare.

Josei manga has been slow to catch on in the U.S. Viz's short-lived 1990s *shōjo* line, Flower Comics, included work by respected *josei* artists like Keiko Nishi, but it didn't connect with American readers. In 2005, Tokyopop launched a *josei* line called Passion Fruit but released only two titles, the short-story collections *Sweat and Honey* and *Galaxy Girl, Panda Boy*, before canceling it. In 2007, Aurora Publishing, an American branch of *josei* publisher Ohzora Shuppan, launched with more lasting success, starting with Chihiro Tamaki's well-received fashion-industry manga *Walkin' Butterfly*. At around the same time, Harlequin began publishing its romance manga in English. By the end of the 2000s, large manga publishers like Viz, Tokyopop, and Dark Horse had all dabbled in *josei* manga.

In the U.S., *shōjo* manga for older teens is often confused with *josei* manga (sometimes intentionally on the part of the publisher, since *shōjo* sells much better than *josei*) and may attract some of the same audience. Ai Yazawa's *NANA*, a sophisticated soap opera set in the world of rock music, is technically a *shōjo* manga, but its mature themes have made it popular with adult women as well as older teenage girls. *Josei* titles dealing with college students, like Tomoko Ninomiya's *Nodome Cantabile* and Chica Umino's *Honey and Clover*, attract many of the same readers as *shōjo* manga set in high schools.

~ ~ ~ ~ ~ ~ ~ ~ ~

Section 2: Elements and Genres

Josei is often stereotyped as romance fiction in manga form, and there's some truth to it; the majority of *josei* manga deals with romance and relationships, usually in a contemporary setting. Office romance is a common subject. The typical *josei* heroine, like the typical *josei* reader, is often a secretarial "office lady," a teacher, or another common pink-collar profession. One example is Yuki Yoshihara's *Butterflies, Flowers*, about a woman who goes to work as an office lady after her wealthy family loses its fortune. Other *josei* manga offer readers a retreat into fantasy professions with heroines who work in glamorous fields like fashion modeling (Ai Yazawa's *Paradise Kiss*, Chihiro Tamaki's *Walkin' Butterfly*, Erica Sakurazawa's *Nothing but Loving You*) or the arts (Tomoko Ninomiya's *Nodome Cantabile*). *Josei* manga set on college campuses, especially art or music schools populated by offbeat creative types, have crossover appeal with older teens and young adults.

In recent years, *josei* has expanded to include fantasy fiction like Erica Sakurazawa's "Angel" stories and science fiction like Moto Hagio's untranslated *Otherworld Barbara*, in which a young man enters the elaborate dream world of a woman who has been in a coma since childhood. Fantasy and sci-fi *josei* manga, however, are still fairly rare. Historical fiction series, especially dramas set in feudal Japan, have been popular for some time and are still common. One current example is Taeko Watanabe's long-running *Kaze Hikaru* (Shining Wind), about a girl who poses as a boy to join the Shinsengumi, a famous Edo-period samurai corps.

One unusual line of *josei* manga is Harlequin Ginger Blossom, published by the international romance-novel giant Harlequin Enterprises. Since 1998, Harlequin has been licensing manga adaptations of its novels, originally written by American authors but drawn by Japanese artists, for the Japanese market. In 2005, Harlequin began translating these manga into English. The titles were first released in the U.S. by comic-book publisher Dark Horse, then through Harlequin's own imprint. Harlequin divided its manga into two lines: Harlequin Pink, for innocent romances containing nothing more adult than kissing, and Harlequin Violet, for more explicit material. Harlequin now sells many of these titles through the e-book market.

Special Issues

Josei is generally more adult than *shōjo* manga, both in the maturity of its subject matter and its level of sexual explicitness. Whereas most *shōjo* manga only hints at sex (and many *shōjo* titles never go beyond the main characters kissing or holding hands), *josei* manga is often fairly explicit in its depiction of nudity and sex. None of the *josei* manga published in English falls into the category of full-bore erotica or *redicomi*, but most feature some nudity and sex scenes. Other aspects of sexuality are often handled frankly as well; *josei* manga like Ai Yazawa's *Paradise Kiss* feature gay, bisexual, and transgender characters, and several of Mari Okazaki's short stories deal with lesbian relationships, as does Keiko Nishi's classic story "Love Song." Even if no outright pornographic *josei* titles have been published in English, the less explicit *josei* manga may still surprise American readers with their frank attitudes toward sex and sexuality.

Although there's plenty of escapist romance, the relationships in *josei* manga tend to be more realistic, less idealized, and a lot more complex than those in *shōjo* manga; this is manga for women with some degree of relationship experience. Moyoco Anno's *Happy Mania* sardonically follows the romantic and sexual misadventures of a self-centered, none-too-bright twenty-something woman who chases one bad-news guy after another, unwilling to settle for her attentive but boring coworker. (In a refreshing twist on romance tropes, this "nice guy" turns out to be no great catch himself.) Yayoi Ogawa's *Tramps Like Us* deals with a successful journalist whose intelligence, career, and height all intimidate men, and who ultimately questions her own sexist fantasy of "marrying up" to an even more successful (and taller) businessman.

That said, the relationships in *josei* manga can be sexist and stereotypical. Like Western romance novels (think *Fifty Shades of Grey*), they sometimes include romanticized fantasy portrayals of sexual abuse or assault, situations women would hardly find appealing in real life. Yuki Yoshihara's *Butterflies, Flowers*, for example, features a formerly wealthy woman who is put in her place by her new boss (and former servant). His relentless sexual harassment of her is portrayed as sexy or flirtatious, even when she protests, and ultimately leads to romance.

Other *josei* romances turn the tables by putting the woman in charge. The protagonist of *Tramps Like Us* takes in a handsome young homeless man as her "pet," while Erica Sakurazawa's *The Rules of Love* follows a down-on-his-luck guy who shacks up with well-off women. Some *josei* manga touch on the real-life social issues affecting modern women, especially in the workplace, where Japanese women still struggle to escape the pink-collar ghetto and women who report harassment or discrimination usually face harsh reprisals.

Because the art styles and subject matter of *josei* are often similar to those of *shōjo*, it can be easy to confuse the two. In the U.S., the tamer *josei* manga are often marketed as *shōjo*. Viz's Shojo Beat line, for example, includes such *josei* titles as *Kaze Hikaru* and *Honey and Clover*. At times, the line between *shōjo* and *josei* can be bewilderingly thin. Ai Yazawa's *Paradise Kiss* is technically *josei* because it originally ran in an adult magazine (the fashion magazine *Zipper*), while her more recent manga *NANA* is technically *shōjo*, despite arguably being more mature than *Paradise Kiss*.

American publishers are sometimes reluctant to license *josei* manga with explicit sexual material or mature themes out of concern that they could be misidentified as *shōjo* and sold to children (or, more likely, outraged adults). Although spicy workplace sex dramedies are arguably the most popular genre of *josei* manga in Japan today, only a few such titles—including *Suppli, Happy Mania,* and *Butterflies, Flowers*—have been published in English. Most are considered too raunchy to publish in the U.S., at least until the American comics market expands to include a larger adult female audience.

Other manga blur the line between *josei* and *seinen*. Moyoco Anno's *Sakuran* (a historical manga set in the world of feudal courtesans) and *Hataraki Man* (a contemporary comedy about a hard-nosed female magazine editor), for example, are technically *seinen* manga because of the magazines in which they run, but the art styles, themes, and memorable female protagonists wouldn't be out of place in a smart *josei* publication. Some indie/alternative manga artists, like Kan Takahama, also have *josei*-friendly styles. *Josei* may be the smallest of the four manga categories, but it also has the most potential to grow, change, and surprise.

Section 3: Notable Artists

Moyoco Anno

The sharp-witted, darkly funny Moyoco Anno has dabbled in many manga genres over the years—her most popular series in Japan is the *shōjo* magical-girl fantasy *Sugar Sugar Rune*—but specializes in *josei* and women-friendly *seinen* manga. Beyond the previously mentioned *Happy Mania* from Tokyopop is Anno's *Flowers and Bees* from Viz, a wry look at metrosexuality, Japan style. The protagonist of the untranslated *Hataraki Man* is a hard-nosed magazine editor nicknamed "Hataraki Man" (Working Man) by her colleagues because of her single-minded dedication to her career. *Sakuran*, published in English by Vertical, is a historical drama set in the world of feudal courtesans, or *oiran*, focusing on a rebellious girl who is sold into *oiran* training in Tokyo's red-light district.

Anno's early manga are somewhat awkwardly drawn, more interesting for their witty writing than their artwork. Over time, however, she's developed into a lush, stylish artist, and is currently as in demand for her magazine and fashion illustrations as she is for her comics. Many of her manga have been adapted into movies and TV series, unusual for a *josei* artist.

Junko Kawakami

Only one of Kawakami's works, the short-story collection *Galaxy Girl, Panda Boy*, has been translated into English; it was one of the two titles in Tokyopop's short-lived Passion Fruit line (the other being Mari Okazaki's *Sweat and Honey*). This single volume reveals an intriguing creator with a sensuous but witty art style and a fondness for slightly off-kilter, magical realism–infused stories set in offbeat communities. The title story involves a girl coming of age in a strange, New Age-y hippie village, while the long story "Club Hurricane Adventure" takes place in an isolated boarding school inhabited by young people whose parents have apparently abandoned them, leaving them to their own devices. More of Kawakami's work has been published in France, where she currently resides.

Tomoko Ninomiya

Tomoko Ninomiya is best known, both in Japan and in the U.S., for her award-winning, long-running manga *Nodame Cantabile*, a drama set at a college of music. The central relationship is between two music students with opposing styles, one a multitalented perfectionist who excels at his studies and the other an eccentric, disorganized pianist whose gifts lie in creativity and improvisation. Ninomiya based her heroine on a real-life music student with whom she consulted regularly while drawing the manga. A bestseller in Japan, *Nodame Cantabile* has won the Kodansha Manga Award and was a finalist for the Tezuka Cultural Award, the highest honor in manga. It has been adapted into both a live-action TV series and an anime.

Keiko Nishi

Long before *shōjo* manga became popular in the U.S., Viz published a number of short *shōjo* and *josei* stories in its magazines *Manga Vizion* and *Animerica*, including a sampling of work by Keiko Nishi, one of the most popular *josei* artists of the 1990s. These stories were collected in the anthologies *Love Song* and *Four Shōjo Stories* (two of the four are *josei* stories by Nishi). Nishi's loose but attractive artwork, command of mood and genre—her stories include tragic romance, tongue-in-cheek comedy, and introspective science fiction—and unflinching eye for the painful details of human relationships make her one of the standout creators in the field of *josei*. Of her work translated into English, the most notable is "Love Song," a harrowing story of the dysfunctional relationship between a well-meaning young man and a cold, beautiful woman still carrying a torch for her first love, a female high-school classmate.

Mari Okazaki

Okazaki's suggestively erotic stories, illustrated with rich, luscious art (her characters always have deep-set eyes and bee-stung lips), are some of the sexiest *josei* manga available in English translation. Her short-story collection *Sweat and Honey* includes a range of evocative stories: a woman is introduced to lesbian love by her cryptic, catlike cousin; a teenage girl becomes obsessed with her "spinster" career-woman neighbor; two high-school friends retreat into an isolated "kingdom of girls." She excels at depicting intense, complex friendships between women. Her more recent series *Suppli*, which follows the ups and downs of a woman who throws herself into her career after getting dumped by her boyfriend, has garnered praise for both its attractive artwork and its realistic depiction of the life of a modern young woman.

Yayoi Ogawa

Ogawa's *Tramps Like Us* (Japanese title: *Kimi wa Petto*, "You Are My Pet") features an unusual gender-role reversal: heroine Sumire is a successful journalist and dedicated career woman who's into pro wrestling and kickboxing, while her love interest, Momo, is a sweet-tempered homeless male ballet dancer she takes in as her "pet." Although a romance develops between the two, the manga is more about the problems of being a macho woman (or a feminine man) in a society that, for all its modernization, still takes gender roles seriously. Over the course of the series, heroine Sumire is forced to reexamine her desire for a man who's taller, richer, and more successful than she is, especially when a man who fits her requirements appears and threatens her relationship with Momo. Winner of the Kodansha Manga Award, *Tramps Like Us* was adapted into a TV drama in Japan. Ogawa's other *josei* titles include the untranslated *Baby Pop, Candy Life,* and *Kiss and Never Cry.*

Erica Sakurazawa

In the mid-2000s, Tokyopop published six one-volume manga by respected *josei* artist Erica Sakurazawa, an artist of elegant, contemporary stories about young adults in complex romantic and erotic situations. In *Between the Sheets*, the first of her books translated and probably the best known, the friendship between two women turns complicated—and increasingly ugly—after they experiment romantically with each other. *The Aromatic Bitters* tells a sensuous food-themed story about two female friends escaping from their relationship problems to a scenic mountain cabin. *Angel* and *Angel Nest* are short-story collections in which most of the stories involve an angel getting involved in mortal lives. *Nothing but Loving You* is a more simplistic romance about a model who falls in love with a gay male model and tries to turn him straight. In *The Rules of Love*, a directionless young man hooks up with older sugar mamas after getting kicked out of his apartment.

Kan Takahama

Kan Takahama is one of the top artists in the Nouvelle Manga movement, a collaborative group of French and Japanese cartoonists who blend the styles of their respective cultures' comics. Her photorealistic art style, adult subject matter, and fiercely intelligent but often bleak and cynical outlook place her work somewhere between *josei* and alternative manga. Takahama's short-story collection *Monokuro Kinderbook* (Monochrome Children's Book) provides an introduction to her sensibility with a wide range of stories, including two autobiographical pieces. *Mariko Parade* is a collaboration with fellow Nouvelle Manga artist Frédéric Boilet and a semisequel to Boilet's graphic novel *Yukiko's Spinach*, about his relationship with a Japanese art model. *Mariko Parade* deconstructs Boilet's relationship and his objectification of Japanese women by reinterpreting his work through Takahama's more jaded eyes.

Chihiro Tamaki

Like Ai Yazawa's *Paradise Kiss*, Chihiro Tamaki's *Walkin' Butterfly* is the story of a tall, gawky girl who finds her calling as a runway model. Whereas *Paradise Kiss* focuses on fashion as a form of artistic expression and rebellion, *Walkin' Butterfly* is more about the business of the modeling industry, as well as the body issues that drive heroine Michiko to excel as a model and prove she's not an overgrown freak. (At almost six feet tall, she towers over other Japanese women and many men.) Some critics take issue with the manga's relentless harping on Michiko's feelings of inadequacy, while others consider it a realistic portrayal of the insecurity many women feel about their looks. Tamaki's other *josei* manga include the untranslated *Airabuyuu to Ittekure!* (Say I Love You!) and *Konkatsu no Tatsujin* (Expert of Marriage-Hunting).

Chica Umino

Umino's most successful manga, *Honey and Clover*, follows a group of students at an art college in Tokyo, detailing both their personal relationships and their development as artists. At the center of the group are Takemoto, a directionless sophomore who harbors doubts about his future in the arts, and Hagu, an extraordinarily gifted but shy and neurotic artist who looks and acts like a little girl. Umino's cute, understated art makes *Honey and Clover* look more like *shōjo* than *josei*; in the U.S., it was published by Viz under its Shojo Beat imprint. But it ran in Japan in the *josei* magazines *CUTiEcomic, Young YOU,* and *Chorus.* It won the 2003 Kodansha Manga Award and has been adapted into multiple anime and live-action TV shows as well as a feature film. "Chica Umino" is a pseudonym; the creator's real name is unknown.

Taeko Watanabe

A prolific artist and two-time winner of the Shogakukan Manga Award, Watanabe is best known for her historical *josei* manga *Kaze Hikaru,* which has been running since 1997 and is still going strong. Set in the 19th century, at the end of Japan's feudal era, it follows a young woman who disguises herself as a boy to avenge the deaths of her father and brother. She joins a samurai police corps destined (as any Japanese reader would know) to become the Shinsengumi, a famously doomed group of samurai who died defending the medieval shogunate government as Japan opened its ports and became modernized. Although *Kaze Hikaru* is technically a *josei* manga, Watanabe's rounded, simple art style is more reminiscent of *shōjo* manga. In the U.S., it first ran as a serial in Shojo Beat magazine.

Ai Yazawa

Ai Yazawa is primarily a *shōjo* manga artist, but her stylish artwork, sophisticated storytelling, and adult themes place her on the border between *shōjo* and *josei.* Her major *josei* manga, *Paradise Kiss,* originally serialized in the Japanese fashion magazine *Zipper,* is the stylishly drawn saga of an initially introverted high-school girl who falls in with a group of eccentric fashion students at an art college, ultimately becoming their model. In the process, she falls in love with one of the students, the magnetic, bisexual George, and defies her parents to pursue a career in modeling. Most of Yazawa's manga deal with artistic, countercultural bohemians who form makeshift families among themselves. Her current series, *NANA,* follows two best friends both named Nana—one an ambitious rock musician, the other a more traditional girl who just wants a part-time job and a boyfriend—as they move to Tokyo together and get entangled in the music industry.

Yuki Yoshihara

Yoshihara is a prolific artist of *josei* sex comedies. To date, her sole title published in English is *Butterflies, Flowers*, a romance about a woman who is forced to get a job as an "office lady" (a secretarial position common in Japanese companies) after her wealthy family loses its fortune, only to find herself working for a man who was formerly her family's servant. He decides to get his revenge by making her office life into a daily hell, but, inevitably, a romance develops between them. Of all the *josei* manga published in English, *Butterflies, Flowers* is perhaps most typical of the *josei* available in Japan: a soapy plot that wouldn't be out of place in a paperback romance novel, a contemporary white-collar setting, and lots of steamy scenes with the handsome bad-boy hero. Yoshihara's lovely artwork and cheeky sense of humor add interest to the story.

CHAPTER 6

Yuri Manga

by Erica Friedman

Section 1: What Is *Yuri*?

The term "*yuri*" is used to refer to stories that contain romantic or sexual relationships between girls or women or, sometimes more generally, stories with a lesbian character. The history of this term is a little fuzzy, as it is subject to both linguistic drift and fashion. While some people use *yuri* and other terms, such as "*shōjo-ai*" or "GL," as if they have clear distinctions—or as if they are interchangeable—the truth is that the etymology is somewhat fluid, forming a broad continuum of definition and understanding. In other words, what any term means has a lot to do with who is using the term and what they think it means.

History of the Word "Yuri" and Related Terms

In 1973, Itou Bungaku, the editor of *Barazoku*, a gay men's magazine, called lesbians in Japan "the lily tribe"—*bara* is Japanese for "rose" and *yuri* is Japanese for "lily." Hence, gay men were *barazoku*, or "rose tribe," while lesbians were *yurizoku*, the lily tribe. This name was adopted first by many porn manga and *dōjinshi* artists, who then named their lesbian characters "Yuri" or "Yuriko," so that it became a kind of cliché for the genre itself. For instance, one of the most common early pairings in erotic *dōjinshi* were Kei and Yuri from the anime/manga series *Dirty Pair*.

In 2001, the American organization for fans of lesbian manga and anime, Yuricon, adopted the word *yuri* to represent all anime and manga works that included lesbian themes. As they state on their website (http://www.yuricon.com/what-is-yuricon/), "It was time to reclaim the term from porn artists and embrace the beauty of the lily as our own."

As anime and manga fandom grew quickly in the West in the 1990s, the term *yuri* was often, but not exclusively, used to represent explicit stories with sexual relations between women. In short, it was considered to mean "porn for guys." The term *shōjo-ai* (which means "girl love" in Japanese) was proposed by an American fan as an analog for *shōnen-ai*, which was being incorrectly used by American fans as a term for boys' love manga. *Shōjo-ai* was originally used by American fans to refer to stories that contained romantic love between girls. The emphasis was originally on the romantic over the sexual, but this age and content distinction was a convention that was made up by Americans and had no meaning at all in Japan. These terms still have no meaning at all when referring to the content of a manga or *dōjinshi* one might buy.

Publishers sometimes use GL, short for "girls' love" in English. This was created as an analog to the preferred genre term for *yaoi,* which is boys' love, or BL. Creators of f/f stories in Japan—especially within the lesbian community—avoided using "*yuri*" for a long while because of the porn connotation, preferring *Onna no ko x Onna no ko* or *Onna-doushi*. These phrases are slowly falling out of favor in Japan as the word *yuri* takes their place as an indicator of "lesbian-themed animation or comics." When these terms are used, they indicate that the content is by women, for a presumed female audience.

"*Yuri*" is now the most common term used to describe any anime or manga series (or other derivative media, i.e., fan fiction, film, etc.) that shows intense emotional connection, romantic love, or physical desire between women. *Yuri* is not a genre defined by the gender or age of the audience, like the four main categories of manga, but by the perception of the audience. The important thing to remember is that the words "*yuri*," "*shōjo-ai*," or "GL" have no legal weight behind them. They are merely terms that fans and publishers use.

~ ~ ~ ~ ~ ~ ~ ~ ~

Section 2: Visual Themes in *Yuri*

Visually speaking, there are some key points to be aware of when purchasing *yuri*. The main difference between *yuri* and BL (*yaoi*) is that there is no one homogenous audience for *yuri*. Where BL is almost always presumed to be for women, *yuri* can appear in any demographic category of manga. Whether it's a manga for girls, boys, or adult men or women, one can find *yuri* themes, characters, or situations. Each of these categories has a slightly different take on the topic, with special differences in the visual representation.

Yuri *in* Shōjo *and* Josei

It might seem surprising to see *yuri* elements in manga for girls, but it's not at all uncommon. Just as classical *kabuki* has men playing women's roles, musical theater in Japan has a tradition of women playing men's roles. As a result, the cool, competent, cross-dressing female character, or the Girl Prince, is a very common visual element in girls' manga. These characters behave in a masculine way, often hitting on other girls, or saving girls in a princely manner. They may even earn a kiss or two. Because these characters "pass" as boys visually, there's less of a chance that they will be seen as "lesbian" couples. But there's still the chance that they will be seen as underage, since stories set in schools are extremely common for girls' manga.

Recently, there has been a growing number of manga for (and often by) adult women. These will adhere relatively strictly to the styles commonly found in *josei* magazines, so adult women will look like adult women. Nonetheless, there are a few popular *yuri* manga artists who draw even their adult characters with *moe* qualities. This cute-ification means that a character might be said to be 25 years old in the story, but will still look significantly younger. In addition, some of these stories have obvious (if not visually explicit) sex scenes between the women in the story. In *yuri* manga for adult women, nudity is typically tasteful, but it still exists.

Yuri *in* Shōnen *and* Seinen

Yuri is a relatively common element in manga for boys and men. Where boys' manga usually relegate the *yuri* to a lesbian best friend with a crush on the main female character, it's not entirely uncommon to see predatory lesbian behavior in *shōnen* manga series. Breast groping is the most common display of this. Messy kissing and other adolescent behaviors might also be portrayed. Although it is rare to see anything more explicit, extreme sexual or violent behavior can sometimes be implied. Lesbian characters almost always look sexy based on a set of typical tropes of "sexy for boys' manga"—that is, they are shapely, with large (or even overlarge) breasts. In action series, they are clad in skintight outfits. These are classic femme fatale characters who act in accord with the stereotype.

In manga for adult men, it will come as no surprise that there are occasional lesbian scenes. Like most media for adult men, fetishes are usually taken to extremes. Violence and sex tend to be extreme and blatant—big guns, big breasts. Just as with *dōjinshi*, sexual situations are often drawn explicitly with great detail given to secondary sexual characteristics and bodily fluids. On the other hand, manga with this kind of explicit lesbian sex is actually pretty rare, compared with *yuri* in the other gender/age categories.

It is more common to find cross-dressing men functioning as women in adult men's manga than actual lesbian characters. The lesbian characters that do appear often act more like physical embodiments of the male gaze. Sexual harassment of other female characters is not uncommon. Predatory lesbian behavior is a recurring theme.

Yuri *in* Dōjinshi

When a *dōjinshi* is labeled "*yuri*," it almost always means there is explicit sexual activity. Because of the popular trend of cute-ification/infantilization called *moe*— and the fact that so much anime and manga takes place in middle and high school— there is a very high likelihood that any art seen in *dōjinshi* could be perceived as "child porn" by officials. Cat girls, robots, or aliens that "look like" girls still look like girls.

Explicitness in *yuri dōjinshi* often goes far beyond simple sexual situations. Characters with extreme secondary sexual characteristics (oversized breasts and/or pudenda) are not uncommon. Bodily fluids are often unrealistically copious. Sexual positions are drawn to allow a viewer maximum visual access.

In Japan, *dōjinshi* that contain explicit sex must, by law, be labeled as 18+. But with so many *dōjinshi* being scanned and translated by fans, sometimes these warnings get lost. If you are traveling across borders with your computer, or with reading material, you might want to remove that *dōjinshi* before leaving home.

~ ~ ~ ~ ~ ~ ~ ~ ~

Section 3: Conclusion

Despite the fact that the word "*yuri*" now encapsulates any portrayal of lesbian themes or characters in manga, *yuri* as a label maintains its status as "porn for guys" in many minds. With the addition of artistic simplification and infantilization, so common now in manga and anime, very often something labeled *yuri* means "drawings of characters that appear young and female having sex with one another."

The most important thing to remember is that the word "*yuri*" does not have a single fixed meaning that is understood and agreed upon by all or even many parties. Judge each work on its relative artistic merits, the level of salacious or explicit visuals, and what a person not conversant with the artistic and thematic styles of *yuri* might think of the material in question.

CHAPTER 7

Boys' Love Manga

by Shaenon Garrity

Section 1: What Is Boys' Love?

One of the fastest-growing genres of manga in the U.S. is also among the most controversial: "boys' love," romantic or erotic manga featuring male-male relationships. Also known as *yaoi*, BL is written and drawn almost entirely by women and is aimed at a female audience. Manga aimed at gay men, known as *gei comi* or *bara*, exist in Japan, but as of this writing none has been published in English.

Nonfans often find BL surprising and confusing, but it's clearly filling a niche in the American market. When the first BL manga were officially translated in the mid-2000s, American manga fans were already devouring BL through online bootlegs. In recent years, the genre has exploded in popularity.

Boys' love manga emerged in the 1970s via two titles by the legendary artists Moto Hagio and Keiko Takemiya, who shared an apartment at the time. Hagio's *The Heart of Thomas* (1974) and Takemiya's untranslated *Song of the Wind and Trees* (1976) both involve romances between students at all-male boarding schools. Takemiya began *Song of the Wind and Trees* before Hagio began *Heart of Thomas,* but it took Takemiya nine years to convince a publisher to accept the story.

Many early BL-themed manga ran in the magazine *Shōjo Comic*, helping to establish its long-standing reputation as the edgiest of the major *shōjo* manga magazines. *June* magazine, launched in 1978, catered specifically to fans of BL and *bishōnen* (beautiful boy) characters, then exemplified by androgynous rock stars like Robert Plant, David Bowie, and the members of Queen.

In the 1980s, BL crossed paths with the growing underground of *dōjinshi*, or self-published manga. The *dōjinshi* scene was dominated by female artists, and fan comics featuring same-sex romances between male characters from mainstream manga soon became enormously popular. Criticized by nonfans for their plotlessness, these manga came to be called "*yaoi*," an acronym of the phrase *yama nashi, ochi nashi, imi nashi* (no climax, no point, no meaning). Some *dōjinshi* artists later established professional careers, bringing *yaoi* sensibility to mainstream manga.

Today, BL-themed manga magazines abound, the most popular of which include *June* and *Be x Boy*. Most BL magazines are produced by small publishers, although some mainstream *shōjo* magazines have their own BL spinoffs. Many BL manga are published directly as graphic novels without being serialized in magazines.

BL in Mainstream Manga

In Japan, BL is seen as a subgenre enjoyed mainly by nerdy fangirls. Geeky female manga fans are sometimes called *fujoshi*, "rotten girls," a reference to their dirty-minded interest in BL. However, BL themes are popular enough to have worked their way into mainstream manga.

Shōjo manga set in all-boys' schools, often with hints of sexual tension between the students, have been popular since the 1970s. The cute high-school boy who attracts crushes from his male classmates is an eternally popular trope. Mayu Shinjo's *Ai Ore!* (Love Me!), for example, involves the relationship between a tough girl who is the "prince" of her girls' school and a pretty boy who is the "princess" of his boys' school.

Male cross-dressing is a common form of fanservice in *shōjo* manga, although, like real cross-dressers, cross-dressing manga characters are often heterosexual. A typical example is *Heaven's Will*, by Satoru Takamiya, in which the male lead, a teenage exorcist, just happens to enjoy wearing women's clothing. Mikiyo Tsuda's *Princess Princess* takes the concept to its extreme with an all-boys' school where certain boys are selected to cross-dress as girls.

Even manga ostensibly aimed at male readers often include BL fanservice. This is especially true of manga published in *Shōnen Jump*, which has a large and loyal female readership. The hit *Shōnen Jump* manga *Death Note* hints at sexual tension between its sexy male rivals, while in the first volume of *Naruto*, Naruto and his male classmate Sasuke accidentally kiss. Goth-themed *shōnen* manga like Yana Toboso's *Black Butler* also tend to attract female readers; *Black Butler* rewards its *fujoshi* fans by playing up the close relationship between the handsome title character and his young male charge.

BL in the U.S.

American fans were first exposed to BL in the 1980s, when a fan translation of Yasuko Aoike's *From Eroica with Love*, a deliberately campy BL sendup of James Bond–style thrillers, circulated at sci-fi and comic-book conventions. By the 1990s, although no BL had been published in official English translation, the genre had inspired a fanzine, *Aestheticism*, which began publication in 1996 and launched the website Aestheticism.net a year later. In 2001, the first Yaoi-Con, a convention devoted entirely to BL, was held in San Francisco.

As online manga fandom grew, unlicensed fan "scanlations" of BL titles proliferated on the Internet. Witnessing the popularity of these online bootlegs, American publishers recognized a market. In 2004, Central Park Media launched a BL imprint, BeBeautiful, with the manga *Kizuna* and *Golden Cain*, and DMP announced its own BL imprint, Juné. At the same time, publishers in both Japan and the U.S. began to crack down on scanlation sites, with mixed success.

Today, many American manga publishers handle BL titles. To avoid parental concerns, most publishers are careful to keep their BL imprints separate from their other titles. Examples include DMP's Juné, Viz's SuBLime, and defunct publisher Tokyopop's Blu.

~ ~ ~ ~ ~ ~ ~ ~ ~

Section 2: Controversial Content

By its very existence, BL is a controversial genre. Whether it's the frank (if idealized) portrayals of homosexuality, the visual depictions of male nudity and sex, or the very idea of erotica aimed at girls and women, there's plenty in BL to cause alarm.

The actual sexual content varies from chaste relationships in which the characters may not even kiss to graphic pornography (although, in accordance with Japanese censorship traditions, genitals are almost always obscured or whited out), causing further difficulty in gauging the age appropriateness of BL titles.

In 2007, *The Consumerist* published an article attacking BL manga entitled "Walmart and Target Sell Anime Porn." The article got several details wrong: the titles in question were not anime, but manga-style comics by American creators. Walmart, a conservative chain that often requires publishers to provide censored versions of potentially controversial music, books, and comics, quickly yanked the offending titles.

Even people who consider themselves liberal about LGBT issues and comfortable with erotic material may be troubled by some of the themes in BL. For one thing, BL relationships tend to be surprisingly retrograde. Couples usually pair off into a dominant *seme* (attacker) and submissive *uke* (receiver); the *seme* is tall, aggressive, and masculine, while the *uke* is petite, timid, and feminine. In other words, the relationships in BL are often just same-sex versions of ultra-traditional male-female relationships. BL manga in which the characters don't form any kind of clear dominant/submissive relationship, like Youka Nitta's *Embracing Love*, are rare.

Some feminist BL fans criticize the sexist subtext of BL relationships and the negative depictions of female characters—who, if they appear at all, are often shrewish stereotypes plotting to break up the central couple. On the blog Yaoi911, writer Alex Woolfson discussed sexism in BL, asking, "Is it enough to have a plucky and capable female best friend or is that just as insidious as the sexless and funny gay best friend stock character in Hollywood movies?" Ironically, the early BL artists of the 1970s tackled same-sex relationships in part to demolish traditional gender roles. Moto Hagio called BL a "first step toward true feminism."

On a darker note, the "forbidden love" element of BL sometimes extends to scenes of torture, rape, and abuse. Few graphically violent BL have been published in English, but it's not uncommon for available titles to involve abusive behavior and/or coercive sex, if not outright rape.

Yaoi featuring young or young-looking boys, called *shotacon*, represent a sizable subgenre in Japan, although few *shotacon* titles have been published in the U.S.—and those that have, like Mako Takahashi's *Almost Crying*, are mostly innocent romances where the characters do little more than kiss. However, relationships between teenage boys and adult men, often teachers or other authority figures, are common.

The depictions of homosexuality in BL tend to be fantasies with little connection to the lives of actual gay men. As manga critic Jason Thompson put it in a 2006 blog post, "There's usually just enough acknowledgment of gayness for there to be a faint feeling of forbidden love, but not enough for any kind of political statement or even self-identification." It's rare for BL to include issues that might affect real-life gay couples, like dealing with homophobia, coming out to family and friends, or interacting with gay culture (which is still largely underground in Japan). Some gay and lesbian BL fans enjoy the fantasy of a world where homosexual relationships are the default, but others criticize the objectification of gay men and unrealistic depictions of their lives. In 2008, blogger and BL fan Isaac Hale sparked an online debate by complaining that, as a gay man, he felt objectified by the female fans at Yaoi-Con.

~ ~ ~ ~ ~ ~ ~ ~ ~

Section 3: Notable Artists

Moto Hagio

Moto Hagio's 1974 manga *The Heart of Thomas*, about the tumultuous relationships between students at a German boys' school, was one of the first BL-themed manga. Many of Hagio's other manga have BL or gender-bending themes. Her science-fiction manga *A, A'* involves a same-sex relationship, and her classic short manga *They Were Eleven* includes a relationship between a male human and a hermaphroditic alien who must choose whether to become male or female.

Akimi Yoshida

Akimi Yoshida's 1980s BL-themed manga *Banana Fish* is one of the most beloved *shōjo* manga in Japan. Set in the gritty world of New York street gangs, it revolves around the relationship between Eiji, a Japanese reporter, and Ash, a gang leader and former rent boy searching for the secret to the drug that destroyed his brother's life in Vietnam. With its violent story line and no-frills artwork, *Banana Fish* is an atypical BL manga, but one with a passionate following.

CLAMP

The four-woman team CLAMP started as a *dōjinshi* circle and often draws mainstream manga with BL themes. CLAMP's work seldom features overt sex or romance, instead dwelling on suggestive, intense relationships between handsome male characters. CLAMP titles with BL elements include *Tokyo Babylon, X, Wish,* and *Legal Drug.*

Yun Kouga

Another artist who made the leap from *dōjinshi* to professional publication, Yun Kouga established herself in the 1980s with *Earthian*, about two male angels who fall in love while stationed on Earth. Kouga's more recent series *Loveless*, a *shōjo* manga with BL themes set in a world where people are born with cat ears which disappear when they lose their virginity, is very popular in the U.S.

Sanami Matoh

Matoh's *FAKE*, the first BL manga published in official English translation, is still well loved by American BL fans. New York cops Ryo and Dee have been partners for years, but when Dee is kidnapped, they realize they're in love. Matoh's other BL manga include *Until the Full Moon*, about a half-vampire, half-werewolf who changes sex during the full moon and finds himself betrothed to a sexy male vampire. Kodaka Kazuma (see below) is one of Matoh's former students.

Kodaka Kazuma

Kazuma is best known for her series *Kizuna: Bonds of Love*, one of the first BL manga translated into English. Two teenage kendo students fall in love, but their developing relationship is tested when one boy learns that his family has ties to the *yakuza*. Kazuma's *Kimera*, a horror BL about a man who falls in love with a dangerous, androgynous vampire, is also available in translation. Unlike many BL artists, Kazuma seems to have an interest in real-life gay issues; the notes in her manga mention clubbing with gay friends and receiving gay-positive fan mail. "I made two guys go through something that's difficult for a straight couple," she writes in *Kizuna*, "so that's probably why I get letters saying, 'Being gay is good!'"

Hinako Takanaga

Takanaga's work is standard contemporary BL done well, with well-developed characters and attractive art. *You Will Fall in Love* and its sequel, *You Will Drown in Love,* are set in the world of professional archery. *Love Round!!* is a romantic comedy about two boxers who fall in love at the gym. Takanaga's most popular title, *Little Butterfly,* is a slow paced but sensitively written series about the relationship that develops between two male classmates.

Youka Nitta

Nitta's soapy, often funny melodramas feature chiseled male leads who defy the typical *seme/uke* stereotypes. Her works include *Embracing Love*, about two adult-film stars who discover they have off-camera feelings for each other; *Casino Lily*, set in the world of high-stakes gambling; and *The Prime Minister's Secret Diplomacy*, a BL political thriller. In 2008, Nitta confessed to copyright infringement when fans discovered that some of her artwork was traced from magazine advertisements. Nitta canceled a planned appearance at Yaoi-Con in the U.S. and subsequently retired from manga.

est em

Maki Satoh, who draws BL under the pen name est em, was a student of *shōjo* manga scholar Matt Thorn, who later oversaw the translation of some of her work into English. Her bold, fluid artwork, sophisticated storytelling, and colorful settings make her one of the most arresting current BL artists. est em's short manga collections include *Seduce Me after the Show*, in which all the stories are set in the world of theater, and *Red Blinds the Foolish*, with stories connected by the theme of Spanish culture. Her one-volume *An Age Called Blue* follows a rock musician with an unrequited crush on one of his bandmates.

Fumi Yoshinaga

The supremely witty Fumi Yoshinaga is best known for *Antique Bakery*, a dramedy about the all-male staff of a patisserie. Ono, the head patissier, is a "gay of demonic charm" who can seduce any man—except Tachibana, the handsome owner, who is immune to his powers. Yoshinaga herself does not consider the series BL, but the gay themes and romantic tension between the male leads have made it a favorite of BL fans.

Yoshinaga's more sexually explicit BL include *Gerard & Jacques*, a manga set during the French Revolution; *The Moon and the Sandals*, about a teacher-student relationship; and the short manga collections *Don't Say Anymore, Darling* and *Garden Dreams*. In 2009, she won the prestigious Tezuka Cultural Award for her non-BL series *Ōoku: The Inner Chambers*, set in an alternate history where medieval Japan developed into a matriarchy led by female shoguns.

CHAPTER 8

Untranslated and Fan Translated

by Erica Friedman

Section 1: A Brief History of *Dōjinshi*

In the mid-1970s, manga and anime fandom in Japan was on the increase and some of those fans felt the need to spend more time with the characters they loved. Fan art and fan fiction were growing rapidly in popularity and, in 1975, an event known as Comic Market—Comiket, for short—was formed to allow fans of anime and manga series to share these derivative works with other fans.

Dōjinshi are small press and self-published comics sold at a number of events around Japan. Although most of what Western fans see of *dōjinshi* are derivative works based on popular anime, manga and games, *dōjinshi* events are also a popular way for young and niche artists to gain a following and experience. While derivative *dōjinshi* are using copyrighted material, they are not typically discouraged by Japanese copyright holders. They are seen as a way to expand and increase the popularity of a series and, as long as the artist sells fewer than a certain number of books, they are not considered to be a financial liability to the copyright holder.

Thematic Elements of Dōjinshi

Because the large majority of *dōjinshi* are derivative, they are often devoted to explicating implied relationships between characters in a series. This is often expressed through explicitly sexual stories. Most of the *dōjinshi* that is shared on Western servers falls into these categories. Depending on the series being parodied, the sexual relationships may be opposite or same sex, they may be intergenerational, or they may contain characters identified as under the age of majority in the series. These last, known as *"lolicon"* (short for Lolita Complex) can present special problems in the case of Western fans who download, share, or transport them. And as discussed previously, *moe*, the current trend of simplified, cute-ified, even infantilized art, means that even characters identified as adult in the series may be childlike in appearance.

Not all *dōjinshi* are sexually explicit, but it's safe to assume that a zip file of scanned *dōjinshi* from Comiket will include at least some explicit graphics in the mix.

Some professional artists create *dōjinshi* of their own characters. This provides a certain legitimacy to their work in Japan, but it confers no such legitimacy to that material in the West. Border guards and airport security are unlikely to be moved by statements that the artist of the series drew that *dōjinshi*. They are looking at the visual content only, not the legality of the item.

~ ~ ~ ~ ~ ~ ~ ~ ~

Section 2: What Are Scanlations?

Previous sections of this book have referred to "scanlations" (also written "scanslation"), a portmanteau of "scanned" and "translation," or "scans" for short.

Scanlations are any work that has been digitally scanned into a computer and translated by fans for digital distribution. Typically, this is done without the approval or knowledge of the creator. Digital distribution has become so easy that many manga fans do not realize that scanlations available online are not legitimate, or that distribution of this material has a negative effect on the market for the source material.

Because so many more people download scanlations than purchase manga, it's more likely for a person to have illicitly obtained downloads on their electronic devices than it is for them to be carrying the physical property. Most Western fans never see a real *dōjinshi*, even if they have large files of *dōjinshi* scans on their computer.

Fan scanlations have no legal standing of any kind. They are always a violation of the original creators' and publishers' copyrights and, if they are scans of material that has been licensed and published in English, they are in violation of the localization and distribution company's copyright as well.

More importantly, scans are a frictionless way to share explicit material across different devices. Because computer files are subject to search at country borders, electronic files of scans of manga and *dōjinshi* are as likely to be searched as physical books. Without the filter of North American publishers, scanlations are more likely than licensed manga to contain vulnerable content. In particular, genres featuring child characters in sexually suggestive or explicit situations, rarely licensed for release in the West, are easily accessible online and may pose the greatest legal risk for readers.

Special Note on Bara

Bara, as discussed briefly in the *yuri* and BL sections, means "rose" in Japanese. Manga and *dōjinshi* drawn by gay men for gay men is referred to collectively as "*bara*." Although *yaoi*/BL is widely available in English and translated *yuri* is slowly but steadily growing, *bara* has not yet been licensed or legally translated here in the West. Most fans will only encounter it as digital downloads and scans. *Bara* mostly contains stories of what in the West are referred to as "bears." These are large men, often hairy and usually portrayed with unusually large sexual organs. *Bara* is mostly extremely explicit and has a higher likelihood of being targeted as both obviously pornographic and homosexual in nature.

CHAPTER 9

Challenges

by Robin Brenner and Shaenon Garrity

Section 1: Challenges in Libraries

When libraries, booksellers, and schools highlight Banned Books Week every October, what these institutions are highlighting is not typically book banning, with the bonfires and protests banning brings to mind, but the much more common formal challenges to titles within their collections. These challenges are requests for the removal of a title from a collection, frequently due to questioning its appropriateness for the intended audience or for collection in a library.

Libraries contend with all manner of challenges, from charges that a title is derogatory or insulting to a particular group to charges that a title contains content deemed inappropriate for either all or some library users.

In recent years, the majority of challenges stem from the concern that a title is inappropriate due to its content, whether it be sexual, violent, or alternative in its presentation of sexuality or gender, for an age group the library serves.

In a public library, there are general age distinctions made between children's, teen, and adult collections, with some libraries further differentiating between, for example, middle-school and high-school ages. Titles are thus most often challenged to be removed from a particular collection or from the library's shelves for fear that patrons younger than the intended audience will check them out. Sometimes challengers may request that a title be moved to another section—from teen to adult, for example—or a library may consider a move as an option that will satisfy the challenger's concerns but keep the title generally available.

In a school library, the rules for both selection and grounds for challenge are narrower. While a public library has the opportunity to move a title, a school library does not, and because of this, with shrinking budgets and watchful administrators and parents, school librarians are very careful in their selections. School collections are primarily intended to support the school's curriculum, and as teachers and staff work *in loco parentis* there is more direct concern that collections fall within what the parents find educational and appropriate for their children.

Collection Development

The reasons for a reconsideration process are simple: every library has a stated mission to provide information and entertainment to the population they serve. A collection development policy is a written document that shows how they select titles for their collection and provides guidelines for selectors. This policy generally reflects the mainstays of a library collection: freedom of information and the freedom to read, as reflected in the Library Bill of Rights stated by the American Library Association. These ideas are at the heart of every library, and every library should have a formal collection development policy on file that states how they select titles for their collection.

The ALA maintains general resources for librarians facing challenges, including:

The Freedom to Read Statement (ALA)
http://www.ala.org/offices/oif/statementspols/ftrstatement/
freedomreadstatement

Intellectual Freedom Manual (ALA)
http://www.ifmanual.org/

When someone challenges a title's appropriateness, staff immediately refer to the mission of the library and the collection development policy to consider the challenge and to defend their choice. Whatever the specific challenge may be, the mission and policy should outline the selection process and delineate the reasons the library might have selected a particular title. Collection development policies frequently show where and how librarians read reviews for titles and the expected merits any title should have to have to gain a place on the shelves.

Unfortunately, many libraries do not have or maintain an up-to-date collection development policy, and when a challenge arises, the lack of clear procedure makes it especially difficult for an institution to defend its choices. When librarians in Marshall, Kansas, were faced with a challenge to two of their graphic novels, Alison Bechdel's *Fun Home* and Craig Thompson's *Blankets*, they discovered too late the vital importance of having a clear collection development policy. When townspeople challenged the inclusion of these titles in their public library collection, the library and town ended up extending the challenge review for months while the library staff composed a collection development policy that should have already been in place.

The Process of a Challenge

Challenges are presented to an institution in a few ways. Many challenges are verbal, presented in person or over the phone, and unless the challenge escalates into a formal challenge, these challenges are usually resolved in conversation and may be uncounted as official challenges.

Verbal challenges can arise because of simple misunderstanding. In the case of comics and manga, this can be as simple as a patron not realizing that comics titles are being shelved in a particular section because teens are their intended audience. If the shelving or geography of the building is not clear to them, and they think of comics as being mainly for children, they may wonder how teen titles are considered okay for five-year-olds. With this kind of challenge, the librarian can explain the reasoning behind the collection and once the intended audience is clear, that person will drop their challenge.

Verbal challenges can escalate into a formal challenge, or a written challenge may be sent to the library without any previous signal of a challenge. Challengers are customarily given a request for reconsideration form to fill out in order to formally present a challenge to the institution.

Requests for reconsideration generally consist of:

- A request for the challenger's contact information
- The title and author information for the challenged title
- A request (or requirement) that the challenger read the complete work

- An explanation of the person's challenge including specifics about their concerns
- A brief explanation of the library's mission and its policy on how the collection is developed
- An assurance that their concern will be addressed as soon as possible, with the procedure for that specific library's reconsideration explained
- Contact information for the library administration if the challenger wishes further explanation

Challengers may or may not include all information in their formal challenge, but this information is requested for staff to be sure they understand the person's challenge before proceeding with reconsidering the title in question.

Ideally the reconsideration process involves staff and community members, and may include the librarian who originally selected the title, the director of the library and other administrators, a town representative, a parent representative, and a school representative. The judging group allows as much time as they can for a thoughtful reconsideration process. The selecting librarian will be prompted to explain the original reasons behind selecting the challenged title, providing background information on the title such as reviews, any relevant awards, author biographical data, and a summary of how other libraries shelve the same title in comparable communities or institutions. Everyone on the committee is usually requested to read the challenged title.

The group meets to discuss the title in terms of the challenge and in terms of possible solutions, such as keeping the title as shelved, moving the title to a different collection, or the serious decision to withdraw the title from a collection. Sometimes the challenger is invited to present his or her concerns in person, but the committee may meet privately. Some also schedule public meetings to gather input and responses directly from the community. Once the committee has reached their decision, they inform the challenger in writing of their decision.

The progression described is very much the ideal of how this process should work. As anyone keeping track of challenges knows, however, these procedures are not always followed by either the challenger or the institution. Sometimes a challenge is made directly to an administrator, who then circumvents the formal process by deciding alone the fate of the challenged title. Sometimes a challenger bypasses the institution entirely and takes a challenge directly to the press or to local politicians. This undoubtedly undermines the goals of the official procedure and results in the library and librarian being on the defensive publicly and often without much warning. Unfortunately this escalation too often leads to misunderstanding and the collapse of the library's original procedure.

When the reconsideration process is circumvented, the institution has a much harder time making its case. News reports and political responses rarely consider the ideals that libraries uphold—the freedom of information and thus the freedom to read for all members of the community served—and become inflammatory very quickly. When the public hears about a challenge to a title in a local school or library in the news, most likely the challenge has escalated beyond the reconsideration process.

Internal Challenges

One less public (but no less significant) type of challenge to manga can come from within the library. Objections from staff do not necessarily follow the same path as external challenges, and the lack of a formal process can make internal objections harder to fight when professional, personal, and political concerns enter the mix.

Nonetheless, the tactics for fighting an internal challenge to a title are much the same as fighting an external one. Education about the format will be just as important, but at least the challenger and the staff will be coming from a common understanding of the purpose and breadth of a library collection.

Another less obvious type of challenge is the challenge that never happens at all because a library chooses not to collect an item a patron or staff member has requested or suggested for the collection. In this case, going back to the collection development policy will be vital in presenting a case as to why a title should be included. Every library has the necessary right to be able to decide what is and is not collected, but if a staff person feels a title is not being collected due to the fear of a challenge or objections not in line with the collection development policy, she or he has every right to advocate for that title and request the title's purchase be reviewed.

~ ~ ~ ~ ~ ~ ~ ~ ~ ~

Section 2: Reasons for Challenges

In a library or school, as with almost any institution, titles may be challenged for a variety of reasons, but the most common seem to be:

- Inappropriate content including language, violence, sexuality, and sexual acts
- Offensive content including derogatory, racist, and/or hateful images and text
- All of the above in specific because they are deemed inappropriate for the intended audience
- Misrepresenting or skewing factual information, including history or biography

Because manga is a visual medium, challenges are often about images. U.S. culture tends toward the belief that images have a stronger immediate impact than words—if you see a shocking image, it's believed to be harder to shake or ignore than the same thing described in words.

The visual nature of manga is thus a double-edged sword. On the one hand, it's easier for selectors and readers to flip through a manga title and see whether a title is appropriate for the intended reader. On the other hand, it's equally as easy to flip through a manga and catch an image or sequence out of context, be startled or shocked by the content, and challenge the title's appropriateness for the reader or the collection.

The majority of challenges to manga are due in part to the concern that the titles are inappropriate for the intended audience. Japanese manga is no more susceptible than prose works to challenges based on audience appropriateness, but because of its visual nature it can be more difficult to defend.

Librarians should be prepared to educate both colleagues and the public at large about the traditions and tropes in the visual style of manga. The information may not resolve the challenge, but the understanding of these conventions can nonetheless go a long way toward demystifying the origins of concerns.

Character Design

The visual style of manga can also lead to quite a bit of confusion about intended audiences and appropriate content. The cute character designs of a title like *Higurashi: When They Cry* may lead U.S. readers to think that the intended audience is elementary- or-middle-school-aged readers when in fact this horror title is aimed squarely at older teens. Characters with round faces, giant eyes, and diminutive stature read as children to readers not used to Japanese conventions of character design, and inexperienced readers may thus think characters who are canonically in their twenties appear to be children or young teens by their proportions.

This is especially troubling to new readers when characters who, to them, look like children end up in decidedly adult situations. Sex and violence appearing to involve young characters are particularly unnerving, and readers with no experience as to how manga creators indicate age through subtle differences in eye shape, height, jaw lines, and facial structure can misread a character's age very easily.

There are times when artists are intentionally pushing boundaries by featuring young or young-looking characters in more mature situations. In Yun Kouga's popular manga *Loveless*, for example, the 12-year-old protagonist Ritsuka is undoubtedly drawn to the college-age art student Soubi for love and support in his confusing and suddenly violent world. Soubi returns his affection with cuddles and touches that walk a very fine line between being affectionate and being sexual. Ritsuka looks like the child he is, and Soubi's college friends question the appropriateness of this intense friendship. The themes Kouga highlights in *Loveless* clearly interrogate sexuality in society and power in relationships, but the age gap between the characters is unsettling.

Nudity

Nudity causes negative reactions in part because there is a cultural gap in what is considered appropriate for younger readers in Japan and in the U.S. Nudity in Japanese comics is seen as an ordinary, natural state. If you take a bath, you're going to be naked. In a U.S. comic, that bath water will be opaque, whereas in a Japanese comic, the water will be clear. Japanese creators are also fond of using nudity as part of humor—embarrassing situations involving sudden nudity are meant to provoke a sympathetic giggle—which makes some readers uncomfortable.

The most famous example of this kind of humor being red flagged is with Akira Toriyama's *Dragon Ball*. *Dragon Ball* features bouts of over-the-top humor, and the lead character, the little boy Goku, runs around naked and naively investigates just why girls are different. Goku's complete ignorance of propriety is part of the joke, and while nothing sexual happens, the manga series has been repeatedly challenged in libraries and schools in the U.S. when readers discover the jokes and pratfalls that involve nudity. As many parents and kids were familiar with the *Dragon Ball* series from having seen an edited version of the anime adaptation on television, they were unprepared for the more risqué content included in the manga.

Sexuality

Sex and sexuality are no more or less discussed or shown in manga than in other comics, but concern arises because the challenger doesn't expect sex or sexuality to come up in a format commonly perceived as being aimed at young readers, or because the challenger believes the content is too explicit for the intended audience. Once again, the differences between what is appropriate for an age in Japan and what is appropriate for the same age in the U.S. can cause problems. U.S. publishers work hard to rate and annotate their titles with U.S. sensibilities in mind, but it's important to be aware that as with nudity, sexuality is considered by Japanese creators and readers to be natural and not something that needs to be hidden from younger readers. Explicit depictions of sex are still very much the domain of adult stories and will not appear in children's or teen manga, but what is too explicit is nonetheless subjective. Librarians should think through comparisons with other visual media, including television, films, and video games, when considering the level of appropriateness for specific titles and where they are shelved.

Variations in human sexuality, from characters who express same-sex desire to characters who identify as lesbian, bisexual, or gay, are frequently present in the depiction of relationships in manga. In Japan, being gay, bisexual, or lesbian is not widely considered acceptable, but in the fantasy context of manga, sexuality is often fluid and more fuel for the fire. Same-sex attraction and relationships are treated melodramatically and romantically, as part and parcel of the ongoing drama many manga thrive on presenting. Most characters who express same-sex desire will not actually identify as gay, but are instead drawn to an individual regardless of that person's gender. More often than not, the appeal of this scenario is the added intrigue of "forbidden love," rather than any call for acceptance of same-sex romantic pairings.

This common trope can throw U.S. readers for a loop. In the middle of CLAMP's charming magical-girl series *Cardcaptor Sakura*, there's an acknowledged (if chaste) romance occurring in the background between two male characters. The now-classic teen romance *Only the Ring Finger Knows* contains all the typical loves-me, loves-me-not misunderstandings found in any high-school romance, but the couple in question just happens to be two guys. Like romantic fiction of all kinds, the level of sexual explicitness varies in keeping with the intended audience. As a teen title, *Only the Ring Finger Knows* contains nothing more than a couple of kisses, while Fumi Yoshinaga's *The Moon and the Sandals,* a title aimed squarely at adults, features explicit sex in its two volumes.

Taboos are also addressed in manga, as with any other format, and so incidents of incest or implied incestuous interest are present, as are intimations of attraction from adults for prepubescent children. The Japanese are more likely to openly address the darker side of sexuality, including these taboos, as manga is considered a contained, fictional place in which to explore fantasies. Neither incest nor pedophilia is condoned in Japanese society, but in fantasy it is acknowledged. If a title contains any taboo subject matter, the selector should consider community standards and the treatment of the subject carefully. Most libraries include prose works that portray these subjects and manga should be treated no differently if the work in question is well written, engaging, and in keeping with established collection development policies.

Whatever the sexuality presented, the key is paying attention to publisher ratings and considering what visual media a collection already contains, as well as being prepared to defend a title based on audience and placement within the collection.

Intended Audience

In Japan, manga is aimed at five major markets defined by age and gender, from children through adults. However, as readership is not defined in quite the same way in the U.S. (especially in dividing so clearly by gender), there can be a lot of crossover between audiences and occasionally confusion about which stories are appealing to which audience. Stories for one intended audience in Japan may appeal to a completely different audience in the U.S.

The meticulously researched period romance *Emma* by Kaoru Mori was, in Japan, published for an adult male audience. Initially, this doesn't really compute according to U.S. reader stereotypes; why would adult men want to read about a Victorian lady's maid and her romantic and social melodrama? It's a bit like marketing Edith Wharton costume dramas to men. When the series began to arrive on U.S. shores, women and teenage girls made up the majority of its readers. However, in later volumes, there are visual sequences that remind readers that the intended audience was originally adult men. While much of the romance is portrayed with tentative touches and tense silence, there is also a significant amount of imagery portraying women dressing or lounging around in bed, complete with full frontal nudity and frank references to sex. For female readers accustomed to romance where much is implied but rarely explicitly shown, the nudity and sensuality intended for a male gaze can be a bit startling. Thus, a series that initially seems appropriate for a teen reader can suddenly catapult into adult territory without any warning.

Gender Play

Many manga, especially manga aimed at girls (*shōjo*), play around with gender identity in both humorous and serious ways. The majority of these story lines are similar to Shakespearean comedies: a girl disguises herself as a boy to, for example, meet her favorite athlete and join the track team, as happens in the classic *shōjo* series *Hana Kimi*. Sometimes the gender swap is male to female, as in *W Juliet* when a young man's father challenges him to prove himself as an actor by passing as female for a full year. In a much sillier premise, the three main boys in *Princess Princess* are cajoled into dressing up as beautiful girls at an all-boys school to bring much-needed "beauty" to the population. In these stories, the conflict between a character's true gender identity and his/her disguise is the basis for the series' humor and romantic comedy, from awkwardness in locker rooms to mistaken "same-sex" crushes. By and large, by the end of these series, characters shed their disguises, and are happily paired off in heterosexual romantic couplings to complete the restoration of traditional norms.

That isn't to say that along the way creators don't have a lot of fun playing around with gender stereotypes and challenging what is considered masculine or feminine in society.

Characters who more earnestly express an alternate gender identity are handled with layers that are not quite in line with U.S. definitions or ideas. There are numerous examples of characters who present a gender not in line with their physical sex. While the character of Nuriko in the fantasy epic *Fushigi Yûgi* is biologically male, he presents as a woman as a way to keep the memory and personality of his deceased sister alive in the world. Ultimately, he chooses to embrace his biological sex and live as a man, and it is abundantly clear that the cross-dressing was not an expression of his true gender identity. In the anime *Princess Jellyfish*, the lead male character dresses as a woman in order to annoy his overbearing father, and it is clearly not an expression of his identity. In the light comedy *Ouran High School Host Club*, the protagonist, Haruhi, is a girl who dresses in a boy's uniform and behaves ambivalently towards fellow students naturally concluding she is male. She's not so much actively presenting as male as failing to correct a misperception, but her lack of traditional femininity is a distinct character trait. In each of these series, characters who begin outside the binary gender system follow paths back toward their biologically assigned gender by the conclusion of the story.

It is far more rare for characters to actually be transgender. The exceptions may be both more nuanced than in U.S. media and more incidental. When a character identifies as transgender, often the expected response from other characters is along the lines of acceptance of a quirk. For instance, in Fuyumi Soryo's classic romance series *Mars*, the brash but helpful upstairs neighbor of the series' male lead, Rei, is portrayed as a cheerful transvestite. Her gender identity and sexual identity are shoved to the side to instead focus on her providing comic relief and a big sister's wise advice to the romantic leads.

A more realistic look at a transgender character can be found in Ai Yazawa's *Paradise Kiss*, in which one of the group of fashion students, Isabella, is a transgender woman. Her identity is never treated as a joke by her friends, although it's clear that fear of rejection is still an issue when she faces society outside their group. She is dramatically feminine, with the support of her best friend, George (who handmade her first dress), and her femininity is never portrayed as an act, but instead her true self coming through. A more recent import to the U.S., and a rare example of manga with transgender characters in the lead, is Takako Shimura's series *Wandering Son*, which tells the intersecting stories of transgender classmates Nitori and Takatsuki, beginning in elementary school and continuing on through puberty.

Race and Ethnicity

One of the most common questions asked by Westerners new to manga is why the characters "look white." In actuality, most manga characters are so simplified and cartoony that they can represent any race, which may be one reason manga has had so much success internationally. However, the characters are usually intended to be Japanese unless specifically indicated otherwise, and manga is definitely not immune to stereotyping and sometimes outright racism.

Japan has little ethnic diversity compared to most Western nations, and manga artists are sometimes insensitive to other races and cultures, usually more out of cluelessness than a deliberate attempt to offend. The international cast of cyborg heroes in Shotaro Ishinomori's classic *shōnen* manga *Cyborg 009*, which launched in 1961, showcases some of the age-old ethnic stereotypes found in manga. Some are familiar to Westerners, like the stoic Native American Geronimo Jr. and the violent New York gang member Jet (named after one of the gangs from *West Side Story*). Others, like the Chinese pig farmer Chang, represent stock characters specific to Japanese culture. In some cases, modern manga have grown more sensitive in depicting other cultures, but stereotypes and ethnic caricatures are still fairly common.

Non-Japanese Asian nationalities, especially the Chinese, often appear in manga in stereotyped ways. Sexy China girls who wear cheongsams and speak in broken Japanese are common characters, like Shampoo in Rumiko Takahashi's *Ranma 1/2* or Kenji Tsuruta's *Spirit of Wonder*. Mainland Asian countries like China, India, and Tibet are often depicted as mysterious lands of magic and secret martial arts. The potential offensiveness of these caricatures may fly over the heads of American readers, given that American pop culture often indulges in the same stereotyping.

The United States, meanwhile, is often imagined as an urban wasteland where the innocent Japanese visitor is likely to be set upon by gun-toting gangsters, as happens in the opening chapters of Akimi Yoshida's *Banana Fish*. The exception is Hawaii, which many Japanese visit on vacation, and which appears in manga like *Ranma 1/2*, Marimo Ragawa's *Baby and Me*, and Aya Nakahara's *Love*Com* as a laid-back land of surfing and pineapples. Some manga set in America, like Kaiji Kawaguchi's political thriller *Eagle* or Natsume Ono's low-key drama *Not Simple*, show a more nuanced and researched image of the U.S., but many manga simply use America as a safely distant setting for all modern ills, from violent crime to dysfunctional families. Caucasians are almost always drawn with wavy blond hair, blue eyes, and big noses.

People of African descent, unfortunately, don't always get off so easily. In the 1920s and 1930s, the first manga artists, studying Western comic strips and animated cartoons for inspiration, picked up on the exaggerated blackface caricatures of the day and copied them. Blackface characters appear in many early manga, such as Shimada Keizō's *Bōken Dankichi* (Dankichi the Adventurer) and Noboru Ōshiro's *Kisha Ryokô* (Train Journey).

Today, some manga artists, not understanding how deeply offensive these caricatures are in American culture, continue to draw characters with the thick lips, frizzy hair, and cartoonish features of old blackface cartoons. For example, Hiroyuki Takei's manga *Shaman King*, which ran from 1998 to 2004, features an African American character named Chocolove who has a huge Afro and thick white lips. For the English translation of the manga, Viz shaded in Chocolove's lips to make them stand out less. Yoshihiro Togashi's *Hunter X Hunter* recently introduced a character named Ginta with similar features.

Although nonstereotypical depictions of Africans and African Americans in manga are rare, they do exist. Akira Hiramoto's recent *Me and the Devil Blues*, a manga biography of blues legend Robert Johnson, deals thoughtfully with African American culture and the history of racism in America.

Some of the strangest recent debates about ethnic and cultural stereotyping have arisen from *Axis Powers Hetalia*, a massively popular web-to-print manga by Hidekaz Himaruya. The characters in *Hetalia* are human embodiments of the nations of the world, circa World War II, with the three Axis powers as the central protagonists. To a large degree, cultural stereotypes and ethnic jokes are the point of the manga: Germany is stern and hardworking, America bosses people around and eats lots of hamburgers, and so on. *Hetalia* has been most controversial in South Korea, which has a long, bitter history of conflict with Japan. In 2009, the Korean government yanked the *Hetalia* anime from television amid complaints that the Korea character was insulting to their country.

Americans reading *Hetalia* are unlikely to pick up on subtle insults to the Korean people. They will, however, probably notice the Nazi-era uniform proudly worn by Germany. Manga artists are often casual about depicting Nazi uniforms and symbols, sometimes just for aesthetic effect; *shōjo* and BL manga, for instance, occasionally feature characters in sexy Nazi uniforms. For obvious reasons, Japan has a very different perception of WWII than the Western world, and this sometimes unfortunately extends to downplaying or ignoring the Nazi atrocities.

In recent years, however, Japan has grown more sensitive to the issue, and manga artists are more likely to depict Nazis or Nazi-like characters as villains, usually with the swastikas on their armbands altered into crosses or other designs. The many examples include the fascist Vandenreich (Invisible Empire) in Tite Kubo's *Bleach*, the demonic villain Magellan in Eiichiro Odo's *One Piece,* and the demon gang Fairy Tale in Akihisa Ikeda's *Rosario + Vampire*. Increasingly, Nazis are depicted in Japanese pop culture in much the same way they're depicted in American pop culture: as generic bad guys divorced from any deep historical meaning.

In recent years, Japan has experienced an unprecedented upswing in immigration from Korea, China, the Philippines, and Brazil. In some cases this has led to anti-immigrant sentiment and discrimination, especially toward Filipino and Brazilian laborers who are accused of taking blue-collar jobs from Japanese workers. It remains to be seen how Japan's increasing diversity will affect the treatment of race and ethnicity in manga.

Religion

"Who do you think are the greatest characters in history? I teach that the greatest character of all time is Jesus Christ, and the second is the Devil. The third? Buddha."

— *Lone Wolf and Cub* creator Kazuo Koike, in an interview with editor Carl Horn

Most Japanese people practice a cafeteria combination of Buddhism and Shinto, the animistic native religion of Japan. Christianity is uncommon, although not entirely unheard of, and most Japanese know little about Western religion beyond the cultural trappings. Western-style weddings are popular, but the white veils and Christian chapels have no religious significance to the celebrants. Crosses are popular accessories in *loligoth* fashion. Describing manga's often absurd depictions of Western religion, critic Jason Thompson writes that "at their best, they show me familiar things through a strange mirror . . . And it's only proper payback for the distorted representations of Japanese culture churned out by Americans—everyone gets to exoticize everyone else, and we're all happy!"

In Japan, religion tends to be incorporated casually into daily life, and few rituals or icons are totally sacrosanct. Perhaps because of this, religion is often treated in manga in a way that may come off as irreverent to readers from other backgrounds. For example, Hiroyuki Takei's *Shaman King* is an action manga in which "shamans" of many world traditions duke it out in supernatural tournaments. Eventually, almost every religion gets its own shaman representative, and it's revealed that religious figures like Jesus and Buddha were just the top shamans of their day.

Manga artists often incorporate Christian imagery simply because they see it as exotic and interesting looking, in much the same way that Western media may appropriate Buddhist or Hindu imagery. CLAMP's supernatural fantasy *X*, for example, bursts with Christian imagery, references to the Book of Revelation, and even a death by crucifixion, but these are little more than cosmetic details intended to add to the manga's dark, gothic mood. Many goth manga use similar imagery, and of course crosses are de rigueur for manga about vampires. Christian iconography can even appear in contexts that strike Westerners as wildly inappropriate, as in Hiroyuki Yoshina's *The Qwaser of Stigmata*, which mixes Eastern Orthodox Christianity with a fanservice-heavy battle plot featuring breastfeeding fetishism.

Catholic saints periodically crop up in manga. In Yoshikazu Yasuhiko's historical manga *Joan*, a medieval French girl decides to follow in the footsteps of Joan of Arc and retraces her life. Less historically accurate depictions of the saint include Arina Tanemura's *Kamikaze Kaitou Jeane*, about a teenage art thief who is the reincarnation of Joan of Arc, and Kumiko Suekane's *Afterschool Charisma*, set at a high school populated by clones of famous historical figures, Joan of Arc among them. Other Catholic saints get a goofy manga reworking in Toh Ubukata's semihistorical fantasy *Pilgrim Jäger*, which features St. Francis Xavier as a sexy cross-dresser, St. Ignatius of Loyola as a philosopher with magic powers, and a heroine who fights wielding the Spear of Longinus.

Christ himself rarely appears prominently in manga. A major exception is Yasuhiko's *Jesus*, a retelling of the Gospels through the viewpoint of a disciple named Joshua, who is also one of the criminals crucified alongside Jesus on Golgotha. Yasuhiko's treatment of the subject is respectful, although he doesn't depict Jesus as divine, just as a compassionate spiritual leader whose miracles are mostly exaggerated by his followers. A much less reverent (but funny) take appears in Hikaru Nakamura's *Saint Young Men*, a comedy in which Jesus and Buddha share an apartment in Tokyo. *Saint Young Men* is currently one of the most popular manga in Japan, but the Japanese publisher is reluctant to license it in English for fear of offending Western Christians.

Judaism is less commonly depicted in manga, although the mystic imagery of the Kabbalah has been popular with artists, for better or for worse, since its inclusion in the hit 1990s anime *Neon Genesis Evangelion*. For example, the Tree of Life figures prominently in Seishi Kishimoto's *O-Parts Hunter* (whose original Japanese title, *666 Satan*, was changed for American audiences). A more realistic portrayal of Judaism appears in Tezuka's *A Message to Adolf*, a thriller set during WWII which deals with the real-life passage of European Jews through Japan.

Japan has very little direct contact with Islam, and Muslim characters or imagery are rare in manga. In 2008, Muslims in multiple countries protested a scene in the anime version of *Jojo's Bizarre Adventure* in which the villain Dio is seen reading from the Koran. The Japanese animators had chosen Arabic text for the book at random, not realizing that it came from the Koran; the text does not appear in the original manga. The Japanese publisher and animation company immediately yanked the offending episode and removed the text.

More than any specific appropriation of religious iconography, devout Western readers may be offended by the underlying agnosticism or atheism of many manga. "Killing god" plots, in which characters go up against a Gnostic-like evil deity, are so common in manga, anime, and video games as to be cliché. (One can probably thank *Neon Genesis Evangelion* for the popularity of this trope as well.) Organized religion is often conflated with superstitious beliefs like astrology, which is enormously popular in Japan. In general, the Japanese attitude toward religion is much lighter than what many Westerners, especially Americans, are accustomed to.

Japanese publishers are aware of this cultural difference and are often concerned about offending Western religious beliefs. For example, *Saint Seiya* is published as *Knights of the Zodiac* in most Christian countries, including the U.S., due to the Japanese publisher's concern that referring to the heroes as "saints" could offend Christian readers. American manga publishers, sometimes at the bequest of the Japanese licensors, often censor potentially offensive religious material. The American edition of *Death Note* tones down lines of dialogue in which antihero Light Yagami compares himself to God, and the American edition of *Shaman King* removes an image of Christ on the cross.

If nothing else, the Japanese are just as happy to abuse their own religions as those of other cultures. Osamu Tezuka's *Buddha* is a mostly reverent manga adaptation of the life of Buddha, but it also includes action plots and slapstick humor that no Christian cartoonist would dare include in a comic book about Jesus. In 2008, when Kagami Yoshimizu's comic strip *Lucky Star* turned the real-life Washinomiya Shrine in Saitama into a popular destination for *otaku* fans, the shrine responded by constructing an *omikoshi* (a portable Shinto shrine used to carry a god through the streets during festivals) decorated with the *Lucky Star* characters.

The idea of covering a sacred altar with pictures of short-skirted cartoon schoolgirls would be unthinkable to most Westerners, but in Japan it's all in good fun. This fundamental difference in attitudes all but guarantees that, no matter how much publishers try to avoid offending religious sensibilities, manga will, to some readers, at times cross a line when it comes to faith.

~ ~ ~ ~ ~ ~ ~ ~ ~ ~

Section 3: Building Your Defense

If you are presented with a challenge to manga, consider all of the ways this challenge is the same as a challenge to any material in a collection. Consult the Office of Intellectual Freedom's wealth of resources on dealing with challenges, including *Coping with Challenges: Strategies and Tips for Dealing with Challenges to Library Materials*. While defending manga may feel like a new and challenging task, many elements remain the same.

It is important to remember that when a person approaches library staff with a concern, the first thing to do is listen. Whatever the challenge may be, the person wants to be heard and to be taken seriously. A challenge always starts out as a chance for education, and challenges can be defused by presenting a calm demeanor, providing a sympathetic ear, and displaying a clear intention to help.

Remember you are not alone, nor are you the first to have to figure out how to tackle defending manga or comics. Colleagues across the country have been in this situation, and contacting organizations such as the Office of Intellectual Freedom and the Comic Book Legal Defense Fund for information and support can be of invaluable help.

Defending manga titles should be no different than defending any title against a challenge, but there are aspects that make defending manga more complex. Unlike challenges of prose works, explanation and education about the format itself is required, and that draws on different resources.

A good first stop is to turn to *Dealing with Challenges to Graphic Novels*, part of the larger project *Graphic Novels: Suggestions for Librarians* (also available in PDF), created by the National Coalition Against Censorship, the Comic Book Legal Defense Fund, and the American Library Association. This document outlines all of the traditional tactics for defending against challenges but acknowledges the particular challenges of defending comics, and while it was written with librarians in mind, the same ideas can be applied to educational institutions as well.

~ ~ ~ ~ ~ ~ ~ ~ ~ ~

Section 4: The Value of Comics and Manga

Professionals in both libraries and education have been advocating for the inclusion of comics, graphic novels, and manga for decades, and there are treasure troves of resources available to you to help convince administrators, peers, and the public of the worth of these formats.

Consider including the following resources on graphic novels, available online and in print, as supplementary materials in reviewing a challenge:

Articles

"Graphic Novels 101: Reading Lessons" by Hollis Rudiger (*The Horn Book Magazine*, 2006)

"Graphic Novels 101: FAQ" by Robin Brenner (*The Horn Book Magazine,* 2006)

"In a Single Bound: A Short Primer on Comics for Educators" by Drego Little (Johns Hopkins School of Education, 2010?)

Websites

Diamond Bookshelf
http://www.diamondbookshelf.com

Get Graphic: The World in Words and Pictures
http://www.getgraphic.org/

The Graphic Classroom
http://www.graphicclassroom.org/

Reading with Pictures
http://readingwithpictures.org/

Books

Building Literacy Connections with Graphic Novels: Page by Page, Panel by Panel edited by James Bucky Carter (National Council of Teachers of English, 2007)

Getting Graphic!: Using Graphic Novels to Promote Literacy with Preteens and Teens by Michele Gorman (Linworth, 2003)

Graphic novels: A Genre Guide to Comic Books, Manga, and More by Michael Pawuk (Libraries Unlimited, 2006)

Graphic Novels: Everything You Need to Know by Paul Gravett (Harper Design, 2005)

The Librarian's Guide to Graphic Novels for Children and Tweens by David S. Serchay (Neal-Schuman, 2008)

The Librarian's Guide to Graphic Novels for Adults by David S. Serchay (Neal-Schuman, 2009)

Making Comics: Storytelling Secrets of Comics, Manga, and Graphic Novels by Scott McCloud (William Morrow Paperbacks, 2006)

Manga: 60 Years of Japanese Comics by Paul Gravett (Harper Design, 2004)

Manga: The Complete Guide by Jason Thompson (Del Rey, 2007)

Teaching Graphic Novels: Practical Strategies for the Secondary ELA Classroom by Katie Monnin (Maupin House Publishing, 2009)

Teaching Visual Literacy: Using Comic Books, Graphic Novels, Anime, Cartoons, and More to Develop Comprehension and Thinking Skills by Nancy Frey and Douglas B. Fisher (Corwin Press, 2008)

Understanding Comics: The Invisible Art by Scott McCloud (William Morrow Paperbacks, 1994)

Understanding Manga and Anime by Robin Brenner (Libraries Unlimited, 2007)

~ ~ ~ ~ ~ ~ ~ ~ ~ ~

Section 5: Finding Reviews

One major step in defending a manga title is locating backup for the selector's choice. Professional reviews are invaluable in showing the literary and entertainment quality of any challenged title, and defenders should search the following resources for reviews:

Journals

The Horn Book Magazine
Kirkus Book Reviews
Library Journal (LJ)
Library Media Connection
Publishers Weekly
School Library Journal (SLJ)
Teacher Librarian
Voice of Youth Advocates (VOYA)

Because manga is a relatively recent addition to many school and library collections, collecting the expected professionally written reviews needed to defend against challenges can be difficult. The archive of reviews for prose work is retrospective and has far more complete coverage than the same for comics, let alone manga. Still, it's always worth checking these journals, as the majority do currently cover the format.

Professional Websites

While respected professional review sources consistently and increasingly review manga titles, they do not and cannot cover all available titles. Librarians and educators may have to turn to online resources to find reviews of a title. If the above resources do not provide enough sample reviews, try the following professional online sources for reviews to add to your review collections. All of these sites are specifically for and/or from library or education professionals.

Good Comics for Kids (group blog at School Library Journal)
http://blog.schoollibraryjournal.com/goodcomicsforkids/

Graphic Novel Reporter
http://graphicnovelreporter.com/

No Flying, No Tights
http://noflyingnotights.com/

Reading Rants
http://www.readingrants.org/

Industry Websites

While they are not expressly connected to library or education professionals, the following review sites provide in-depth reviews of many manga titles and series and should be considered as additional resources for gathering information on a challenged title.

Guys Lit Wire
http://guyslitwire.blogspot.com/

ICv2.com
http://icv2.com/

Manga Bookshelf
http://www.mangabookshelf.com/

Sequential Tart
http://www.sequentialtart.com/

Awards

Awards for manga in Japan are given out by publishers, rather than one overarching organization, but the titles highlighted by these awards are the cream of the crop when it comes to manga publications.

Kodansha Manga Awards (sponsored by Kodansha since 1977)

Shogakukan Manga Award (sponsored by Shogakukan since 1955)

Tezuka Osamu Cultural Prize (sponsored by the newspaper Asahi Shimbun since 1997)

In the U.S., manga series may win notice in categories among the major comics awards like the Will Eisner Comic Industry Awards, presented since 1988. Since 2007, the Eisner Awards have included a category called Best U.S. Edition of International Material–Japan (apart from Best U.S. Edition of International Material, which covers all international comics and graphic novels) to highlight the popularity and excellence of Japanese manga in the U.S.

Consult Your Peers

In more rare cases, librarians and educators may have to seek impromptu reviews from colleagues who collect and can defend the series. Librarians and educators keep connected through listservs and online forums, and colleagues can be invaluable resources for locating similar communities and polling your peers about the placement of a title within other collections. If you're looking for a more immediate response about where to best shelve a title, for example, check in with these online communities for an immediate snapshot of which libraries shelve what where.

ALA's Graphic Novel Member Initiative Group (Hosted by ALA)
http://connect.ala.org/graphicnovels

COMIX-ACADLIBS (Hosted by Columbia University)
https://lists.columbia.edu/mailman/listinfo/comix-acadlibs

Graphic Novels for Libraries (Hosted by Yahoo)
http://groups.yahoo.com/group/gn4lib/

YALSA-BK (Hosted by YALSA, for YA librarians)
http://lists.ala.org/wws/info/yalsa-bk

Keep It Simple

Avoid using terms or jargon unfamiliar to the general public, especially if you yourself are relatively steeped in terminology. Keep in mind how forbidding unknown vocabulary can be and think about how to explain manga's style, history, and conventions in terms familiar to your audience.

Images vs. Prose

Videos, picture books, video games, and manga are similarly vulnerable to challenges in that, because they are visual, readers may cite different concerns than they would with prose works. Content considered appropriate in prose is often felt to be less allowable in pictures.

In considering how to frame discussions in a common language while handling a challenge, references to the familiar and widespread conventions of movie content and ratings, illustration, and fine art can help everyone reach an understanding of the format under review. Refresh your understanding of the policies and standards governing the library or school's collecting of other visual mediums including picture books, movies, television, and video games.

~ ~ ~ ~ ~ ~ ~ ~ ~

Section 6: Criminal Prosecutions of Manga in the United States and Canada

The Fight to Protect Comics

Comic books have been the object of legal controversy since the 1950s when the Senate Judiciary Committee's Subcommittee to Investigate Juvenile Delinquency investigated the medium in response to public pressure about its content. Those investigations led to the self-censorship regime of the Comics Code Authority.

Comic books have been targeted in American criminal courts since the 1970s, with the New York obscenity conviction of two store clerks who sold *Zap #4*.

A second wave of criminal cases emerged in 1986 when a retailer in Lansing, IL, was convicted of possession and sale of obscene materials for selling adult comics to an undercover police officer.

The Comic Book Legal Defense Fund formed to wage the successful appeal in that case. Since then the organization has arranged and paid for the defense in several cases against retailers, artists, and now readers.

Since 2000, manga has been the target of legal controversy.

Manga Is an International Force

Manga, or Japanese comics, and its sister form of anime, or Japanese animation, are a combined global entertainment phenomenon.

Japanese culture has vastly different taboos about sexual content and nudity, leading to misunderstandings and prosecutions of manga here in North America. With higher popularity and visibility, prosecutions and challenges are increasing in the United States and other countries.

In the United States and Canada, manga culture has exploded to accommodate more than 200 conventions every year, ranging from small, local events attracting hundreds, to national events attracting tens of thousands.

A generation of North American readers has grown up on manga and anime. Manga can be found in every major bookstore, and anime's long presence on television has now extended into the contemporary format of online streaming.

As the generation that grew up on manga become adults, so do their tastes in manga. This is making them increasingly vulnerable to prosecution under American and Canadian law, due to cultural differences regarding the content of manga, and problematic applications of obscenity and child pornography laws.

Manga Prosecutions Have Begun

Since 2000, prosecutions and criminal convictions for manga in the United States have begun. Below we will discuss four:

Texas v. Castillo—A clerk was convicted of selling obscenity for selling manga to an adult.

United States v. Whorley—A reader is convicted for viewing and printing manga of a sexual nature on a public computer.

United States v. Handley—After ordering manga from Japan, a collector pleaded guilty to possession of child pornography for owning manga of a sexual nature.

R. v. Matheson—An American reader faced charges of importation of child pornography in Canada for manga on his laptop. After a two-year, $75,000 battle, the charges were dropped.

Texas v. Castillo

The first court case against manga in the United States began in 2000.

Jesus Castillo, a clerk at Keith's Comics, a comic book store in Dallas, TX, was arrested and charged with two counts of selling obscene materials for selling manga to an undercover police officer. The police officer bought the comics, which were labeled "Not For Children," from the adults-only section of the store.

The titles at issue were translations, in comic book format, of the manga *Demon Beast Invasion: The Fallen* and *Urotsukidoji: Legend of the Overfiend*, both by Toshio Maeda: two popular horror comics containing strong sexual content.

The prosecutor's case hinged on the perception of comics as a children's medium, and the assertion that the manga in question was not art, but was obscenity designed to target youth.

The defense argued that the comics in question are protected Free Expression under the First Amendment.

Dr. Susan Napier, an Asian studies expert, testified regarding the cultural merit of manga, especially with regard to the medium's status in Japan. The status of these manga as part of a larger art tradition was a cornerstone of her defense.

Scott McCloud, comics expert, testified about the artistic merit of the comics at issue, and included statistics demonstrating that a majority of comic book readers in the USA are adults.

A private investigator testified about comparable materials widely available in Texas.

Prosecutors did not offer conflicting expert testimony, only the testimony of the arresting police officer, who is not an expert.

In closing arguments, prosecutors rejected the artistic and cultural merit of both comics generally, and these manga in particular, stating:

"I don't care what type of evidence or what type of testimony is out there; use your rationality; use your common sense. Comic books, traditionally what we think of, are for kids . . . This is in a store directly across from an elementary school and it is put in a medium, in a forum, to directly appeal to kids. That is why we are here, ladies and gentlemen. We're here to get this off the shelf."

The jury sided with the prosecution. Castillo was sentenced to 180 days in jail, a $4,000 fine, and one year probation.

Attempts to appeal the case were unsuccessful. Castillo ultimately served a period of unsupervised probation.

The PROTECT Act of 2003 (§ 1466A)

In 2003, the United States Congress passed the PROTECT Act, a sweeping anti–child pornography law that expanded prosecutorial remedies to punish child sex offenses. Unfortunately, the law also created a new crime—producing, receiving, possessing, or manufacturing "obscene child pornography" of a non-photographic nature.

Child pornography is photographic evidence of a crime where an actual minor is sexually abused. "Obscene child pornography" is a new category that criminalizes a nonphotographic image, such as "a visual depiction of any kind, including a drawing, cartoon, sculpture, or painting" that depicts (i) a minor engaging in sexually explicit conduct and is obscene (§ 1466A(a)(1) and § 1466A(b)(1)); or (ii) an image that is, or appears to be, of a minor engaging in graphic bestiality, sadistic or masochistic abuse, or sexual intercourse and lacks serious literary, artistic, political, or scientific value (§ 1466A(a)(2) and § 1466A(b)(2)).

PROTECT is used to prosecute anime and manga.

U.S. v. Whorley

U.S. v. Whorley was the first case to test manga within the confines of the PROTECT Act.

Dwight Whorley used computers at the Virginia Employment Commission, a public resource, to download manga alleged to depict "children engaged in explicit sexual conduct with adults." He was charged with "knowingly receiving" child pornography for printing out two cartoons, and viewing others, 19 counts in all.

In 2006, a jury found Whorley guilty for "receiving" obscene cartoons, for which he was sentenced to 20 years in prison, with a 10-year probation thereafter. His sentence was aggravated by a previous conviction for receiving actual child pornography. If this were his first offense, he would have been subject to a minimum sentence of "not less than 5 years and not more than 20 years" in prison.

Whorley was sentenced under the same guidelines governing actual child pornography.

U.S. v. Handley

Christopher Handley, a manga collector, was arrested in 2006 after postal inspectors viewed a package of manga he ordered from Japan. After receiving his package at the post office, he was followed to his home and served with a search by federal and local police who seized his lifetime collection of manga and anime—over 1,000 books and magazines, hundreds of DVDs, and seven computers.

Handley was a model citizen with no criminal record. He was a computer programmer who served in the U.S. Navy, was disabled, and took care of his disabled mother in her home. His passions were manga and bible study. He possessed no photographic pornography of any kind.

Handley was a collector of manga as a whole, and the vast majority of manga and images he possessed contained no fantasy representations of minors at all.

When Handley awaited trial, prosecutors did not distinguish between manga and obscene material. They prohibited him from viewing or accessing any manga or anime on the Internet, ordering anime video or written material, or engaging in Internet chat, the latter harming his ability to prepare his defense.

Handley was also forced to undergo mental health counseling.

Unlike Whorley, who was convicted for mere possession of sexual images of minors, the court in Handley found that the images must be found obscene to be convicted.

Despite this one positive development, the government assumed an aggressive posture towards Handley, and ultimately he chose to plead guilty rather than face a mandatory minimum sentence of 5 years in prison.

Court documents show that Handley had no history of criminal behavior, possessed no actual photographic pornography of any kind, and posed no danger to anyone in his community. In sentencing documents, the government argued that the mere possession of graphic manga represented a form of "sexual deviancy" that required imprisonment, to be followed by psychological treatment and supervision.

Handley was sentenced to 6 months in prison, to be followed by three years of supervised release running concurrent with five years of probation, and forfeiture of all material seized by police.

Handley was ultimately convicted for receiving and possessing obscene cartoons for possessing seven (7) books:

- *Mikansei Seifuku Shōjo* (Unfinished School Girl) by Yuki Tamachi (LE Comics)
- *I [Heart] Doll* by Makafusigi (Seraphim Comics)
- *Kemono* for ESSENTIAL 3 (THE ANIMAL SEX ANTHOLOGY Vol. 3) by Masato Tsukimori, et al. (Izumi Comics)
- *Otonari Kazoku* (Neighboring House Family) by Nekogen (MD Comics)
- *Eromon* by Makafusigi (Seraphim Comics)

- *Kono Man_ ga Sugoi!* (This Man_ Is Awesome!) by Makafusigi (Seraphim Comics)
- *Hina Meikyū* (Doll Labyrinth) by Makafusigi (Seraphim Comics)

R. v. Matheson

In 2010, Ryan Matheson, a 25-year-old American citizen, computer programmer, and manga fan was unlawfully arrested and abused by Canadian authorities. He was wrongfully accused of possessing and importing child pornography because of constitutionally protected manga on his laptop—before he was let into the country!

Ryan suffered severe abuse by the authorities. He wasn't properly informed of the reason for detention. He was denied access to counsel and the American Embassy. The search of his property was illegal. He suffered cruel and unusual punishment, including being denied food and blankets. Police transporting him to prison actually said, "If you get raped in here, it doesn't count!"

Like Handley, Ryan had no criminal record, and was not in possession of any photographic material.

Ryan was released to await trial, but one of the conditions was that he was not allowed to use the Internet outside of work at one specific company. For two years his life was frozen under this false accusation.

The material Ryan was accused of possessing was innocuous. One image, "The 48 Positions: Moe Style," is a parody of a famous Japanese woodblock print of sumo wrestling moves. The other was a common *dōjinshi*, or fan-made comic book, depicting a fantasy scenario between nonhuman characters.

CBLDF aided Ryan's defense, which included expert testimony about the artistic merit of manga; the fact that the material he is accused of possessing is protected speech in his home country of the U.S.; and that the material is accepted in its origin country of Japan.

As a result of Ryan's strong defense, the Canadian government dropped all charges against Ryan earlier this year.

In addition to substantive aid, CBLDF assisted Ryan's case financially. Ryan's total legal fees totaled $75,000. CBLDF has contributed $30,000 to those expenses to date, and our colleagues at Canada's Comic Legends Legal Defense Fund contributed $11,000. We are currently fundraising to restore the final $34,000 Ryan was forced to spend defending himself against these outrageous charges. To help us, please make a donation at CBLDF.org.

The Cloud of Self-Censorship

In North America, some customs and law enforcement officials still regard manga as a code word for pornography.

Cartoonists and readers are curtailing the content they carry across borders, fearing harassment or prosecution for carrying comic books that are protected by the First Amendment in the USA. Many of these comics are innocuous.

Academics studying Japanese culture have expressed fear that studying sexually focused manga will make them targets for prosecution.

Artists feel vulnerable carrying digital files across borders if their art is sexual in nature.

Current cases focusing on instances in which people have purchased, downloaded, or otherwise come into the possession of manga that were not available from U.S. publishers, nor were they translated into English, create added vulnerability. Japanese manga are available in the original Japanese for anyone in the U.S. to order through a variety of sources, and in these cases the works that caused legal action were not U.S. editions. This does not diminish the challenge to the protection of the freedom of speech (and freedom to read) nor the ignorance about manga that these prosecutions demonstrate.

Manga Is Protected Speech

Forces urging censorship of manga, in both the United States and Canada, tend to be ignorant of what manga really is. Manga, like comics, is a medium, not a genre, and it encompasses a wide range of expression that speaks to audiences of all ages and interests.

Art is not child pornography. Art provides a safe place for individuals to explore culture, identity, and ideas. Prosecuting individuals for possession of comics does not prevent or punish the sexual abuse of real people.

Manga and comic books are realms of legitimate speech that are protected by the First Amendment.

The Comic Book Legal Defense Fund website offers critical information for American manga fans both at home and traveling abroad, including:

Manga Is Under Attack! Know Your Rights & Protect Yourself!
http://cbldf.org/manga/

Criminal Prosecutions of Manga
http://cbldf.org/criminal-prosecutions-of-manga/

CBLDF Case Files—R. v. Matheson
http://cbldf.org/about-us/case-files/cbldf-case-files-canada-customs-case/

Advisory: Crossing International Borders
http://cbldf.org/resources/customs/advisory-crossing-international-borders/

As part of its core mission, the CBLDF provides financial aid, legal counsel, and legal expertise to individuals being prosecuted for buying, possessing, or traveling with manga.

Resources

Allison, Anne. "The Japan Fad in Global Youth Culture and Millennial Capitalism." *Mechademia* 1 (2006): 11-22 Print.

Allison, Anne. "Sailor Moon: Japanese Superheroes for Global Girls." *Japan Pop!: Inside the World of Japanese Popular Culture.* Ed. Timothy J. Craig. Armonk, NY: M.E. Sharpe, 2000. 259-278. Print.

Brenner, Robin E. *Understanding Manga and Anime.* Westport, CT: Libraries Unlimited, 2007. Print.

Gravett, Paul. *Manga: Sixty Years of Japanese Comics.* New York: Collins Design, 2004. Print.

Isao, Shimizu. "Red Comic Books: The Origins of Modern Japanese Manga." *Illustrating Asia: Comics, Humour Magazines, and Picture Books.* Ed. John A. Lent. Richmond: Curzon Press, 2001. 137-150. Print.

Johnson-Woods, Toni. *Manga: An Anthology of Global and Cultural Perspectives.* New York: Continuum, 2010. Print.

Kalen, Elizabeth. *Mostly Manga: A Genre Guide to Popular Manga, Manhwa, Manhua, and Anime.* Santa Barbara, CA: Libraries Unlimited, 2012. Print.

Kelts, Roland. *Japanamerica: How Japanese Pop Culture Has Invaded the U.S.* New York: Palgrave Macmillan, 2006. Print.

Koyama-Richard, Brigitte. *Japanese Animation: From Painted Scrolls to Pokémon.* Paris: Flammarion, 2010. Print.

Koyama-Richard, Brigitte. *One Thousand Years of Manga*. Paris: Flammarion, 2008. Print.

Lehmann, Timothy R. *Manga: Masters of the Art*. New York: Collins Design, 2005. Print.

McCarthy, Helen, and Osamu Tezuka. *The Art of Osamu Tezuka: God of Manga*. New York: Abrams ComicArts, 2009. Print.

Mechademia. Minneapolis: University of Minnesota Press, 2006–present. Annual. Print.

Nash, Eric Peter. *Manga Kamishibai: The Art of Japanese Paper Theater*. New York: Abrams, 2009. Print.

Nunez, Irma. "Tracing the Genealogy of *Gekiga*." The Japan Times Online. N.p., 24 Sept. 2006. Web. 2 Sept. 2012. <http://www.japantimes.co.jp/text/fb20060924a1.html>.

Ogi, Fusami. "Gender Insubordination in Japanese Comics (Manga) for Girls." *Illustrating Asia: Comics, Humour Magazines, and Picture Books*. Ed. John A. Lent. Richmond: Curzon Press, 2001. 171-186. Print.

Otaku USA. Washington, DC: Sovereign/Homestead, 2007–present. Bi-monthly. Print.

Patten, Fred. *Watching Anime, Reading Manga: 25 Years of Essays and Reviews*. Berkeley, CA: Stone Bridge, 2004. Print.

Robins, Scott, and Snow Wildsmith. *A Parent's Guide to the Best Kids' Comics: Choosing Titles Your Kids Will Love*. Iola, WI: Krause Publications, 2012. Print.

Schilling, Mark. *The Encyclopedia of Japanese Pop Culture*. New York: Weatherhill, 1997. Print.

Schodt, Frederik L. *Dreamland Japan: Writings on Modern Manga*. Berkeley, CA: Stone Bridge, 1996. Print.

Schodt, Frederik L. *Manga! Manga!: The World of Japanese Comics*. Revised ed. Tokyo: Kodansha International, 1997. Print.

Shen, Kuiyi. "Lianhuanhua and *Manhua*—Picture Books and Comics in Old Shanghai." *Illustrating Asia: Comics, Humour Magazines, and Picture Books*. Ed. John A. Lent. Richmond: Curzon Press, 2001. 100-120. Print.

Shiraishi, Saya S. "Doraemon Goes Abroad." *Japan Pop!: Inside the World of Japanese Popular Culture*. Ed. Timothy J. Craig. Armonk, NY: M.E. Sharpe, 2000. 287-308. Print.

Thompson, Jason. *Manga: The Complete Guide*. New York: Ballantine/Del Rey, 2007. Print.

Tsurumi, Maia. "Gender Roles and Girls' Comics in Japan: The Girls and Guys of *Yukan* Club." *Japan Pop!: Inside the World of Japanese Popular Culture*. Ed. Timothy J. Craig. Armonk, NY: M.E. Sharpe, 2000. 171-85. Print.

Wei, Shu-chu. "Shaping a Cultural Identity: The Picture Book and Cartoons in Taiwan, 1945-1980." *Illustrating Asia: Comics, Humour Magazines, and Picture Books*. Ed. John A. Lent. Richmond: Curzon Press, 2001. 64-80. Print.

Weiner, Michael. "The Invention of Identity: Race and Nation in Pre-War Japan." *The Construction of Racial Identities in China and Japan: Historical and Contemporary Perspectives*. Ed. Frank Dikötter. Honolulu: University of Hawai'i, 1997. 96-117. Print.

Wiseman, Paul. "Manga Comics Losing Longtime Hold on Japan." *USA Today*. N.p., 18 Oct. 2007. Web. 4 Sept. 2012. <http://www.usatoday.com/news/world/2007-10-18-manga_N.htm>.

Wong, Wendy Siuyi. "Globalizing Manga: From Japan to Hong Kong and Beyond." *Mechademia* 1 (2006): 23-46. Print.

Wong, Wendy Siuyi. *Hong Kong Comics: A History of Manhua*. New York: Princeton Architectural, 2002. Print.

Yadao, Jason S. *The Rough Guide to Manga*. London: Rough Guides, 2009. Print.

About the
Comic Book Legal Defense Fund

The Comic Book Legal Defense Fund is a nonprofit organization dedicated to the protection of the First Amendment rights of the comics art form and its community of retailers, creators, publishers, librarians, and readers.

The CBLDF provides legal referrals, representation, advice, assistance, and education to cases affecting the First Amendment right to read, create, publish, sell, and distribute comics and graphic novels. We help individuals and businesses who are being criminally prosecuted because of the comic books they read, make, buy, or sell. We help creators who are being attacked in cases where their work is clearly protected as parody or fair use. We help libraries gather resources to defend graphic novel challenges. We are the first line of defense when authorities intimidate individuals or businesses about the comics they read, make, buy, or sell. Often a letter or phone call from the Comic Book Legal Defense Fund's lawyers will end a case before it starts.

http://cbldf.org/